— *live your* —

Best Day Ever

live your

Best Day Ever

THIRTY-FIVE STRATEGIES
FOR
DAILY SUCCESS

ANNE-MARIE FAIOLA

ForbesBooks

Published by ForbesBooks, Charleston, South Carolina.
Member of Advantage Media Group.

ForbesBooks is a registered trademark, and the ForbesBooks colophon is a trademark of Forbes Media, LLC.

Printed in the United States of America.

10 9 8 7 6 5 4 3 2 1

ISBN: 978-0-9983655-4-1
LCCN: 2017941176

Cover design by Katie Biondo.
Layout design by Megan Elger.

This publication is designed to provide accurate and authoritative information in regard to the subject matter covered. It is sold with the understanding that the publisher is not engaged in rendering legal, accounting, or other professional services. If legal advice or other expert assistance is required, the services of a competent professional person should be sought.

Advantage Media Group is proud to be a part of the Tree Neutral® program. Tree Neutral offsets the number of trees consumed in the production and printing of this book by taking proactive steps such as planting trees in direct proportion to the number of trees used to print books. To learn more about Tree Neutral, please visit **www.treeneutral.com.**

Since 1917, the Forbes mission has remained constant. Global Champions of Entrepreneurial Capitalism. ForbesBooks exists to further that aim by bringing the Stories, Passion, and Knowledge of top thought leaders to the forefront. ForbesBooks brings you The Best in Business. To be considered for publication, please visit **www.forbesbooks.com.**

To all my mentors along the way:
my dad; my mom; my business coach, Ron Huntington; Verne Harnish;
and all my many forum-mates from the Entrepreneurs' Organization,
Women Presidents' Organization, and Bellingham Mastermind Group
who taught me so much and supported me through the many ups
and downs. A big thank you to my husband who tolerates my serial
entrepreneur tendencies and fiercely loves our family with unmatched
loyalty. You helped me develop the Best-Day-Ever philosophy
and inspired me to write it down.

Table of Contents

Be Responsible for Your Own Success!
Stop relying on "luck."

Write Your Own Story
Reframe your history to create hope and meaning.

Your Unique Experiences + Your Personal Passion = What the World Needs
Love the circumstances of your life unconditionally.

You Can't Divorce Success from Discipline
Discipline is what makes success look easy.

Success Can Be Systematized
Replicate small victories every day.

Feet First, Not Head First
Small starts can lead to great success.

ABOUT THE AUTHOR

Anne-Marie Faiola is on a fascinating lifelong entrepreneurial and creative journey. She began as a young girl with a hamster-breeding business, and after many interesting twists and turns, has become the well-known crafting industry leader: the Soap Queen. Along the way, she founded and built the Bramble Berry enterprise, which includes a large e-commerce business that sells handcraft provisions, ingredients, and supplies for soapmaking; a popular retail store for supplies and classes; and a real estate investing company. An accomplished innovator and visionary, she is never without a new business venture percolating. She holds an MBA, is a certified nutritional therapist, and is passionate about an always-learning/always-challenging lifestyle. With two toddlers at home, and married to a fellow entrepreneur, her life is full—but she always finds time for reading, baking, hiking, and doing the crafty things that she loves.

FOREWORD

Buckminster Fuller, the great engineer, said, "If you want to teach people a new way of thinking, don't bother trying to teach them. Instead, give them a tool, the use of which will lead to new ways of thinking." In the book you are about to read, that is exactly what Anne-Marie Faiola has done: she has given you a set of tools—thirty-five of them in fact—that will change the way you think about yourself and your life.

You'll find strategies for personal growth, for building stronger relationships, for nurturing your body, and for enhancing your professional success. At first glance, some of these may seem like small things, but do not underestimate their power and usefulness. This is an extraordinary set of tools, one that is as down to earth and easy to use as it is effective and comprehensive.

Using these tools regularly will carve out routines in your daily life and in your habitual thought patterns. It will sharpen your vision for seeing opportunities even in the midst of challenges. You'll discover new creativity and fulfillment, and you will find yourself living the best possible version of your life.

The wisdom you'll find in this book will enhance your professional satisfaction, while at the same time improving all aspects of your life. It's not so overwhelming and idealistic, however, that it's impossible for mere mortals to achieve. Anne-Marie reminds us that baby steps, no matter how small or slow, can eventually travel huge distances. Applying just one or two of these strategies to your life will get you started on a journey toward a happier, more creative, and more prosperous life.

I have known Anne-Marie personally for over a decade, ever since she graduated from the Entrepreneurs' Organization's (EO) "Birthing of Giants" executive program, which I founded and held at MIT. A great student of business, she took the lessons from that program and has used them to scale her business. She also works with one of our Gazelles coaching partners to ensure she is accountable for practicing what she preaches in this book.

Anne-Marie has utilized passion, purpose, and persistence to carve out her successful niche in the business world ("Soap Queen") and scale her life, answering some of the big questions that drive success. She'll share these questions with you and how she answered them for herself and her business, giving this book real-life credibility. Anne-Marie's business is a steady growth machine because she has implanted strategies learned long ago in a consistent manner. Entrepreneurs often go into business for themselves and envision freedom but then find themselves chained to their desks and stuck. Good systems can solve this and give you personal and professional freedom.

Anecdotes from Anne-Marie's life, coupled with inspiring stories from other individuals who have found the keys to success, make this book a fun and easy read. Even more valuable, however, is the way Anne-Marie shows us how to customize her unique toolset so that it will fit our individual needs. Her calls to action can be easily and quickly applied to any life. There is a workbook-like aspect to this book that helps you recognize your own unique gifts and abilities and gives you a framework for utilizing them to benefit yourself, your family, your business, and your community. When Anne-Marie was in class with me, I advocated that she "control the ink" by writing a book. Not only did she do that for her niche of making soap, but she's broadened that idea with this book you hold in your hands.

A successful personal and professional life, birthed out of multiple challenges in Anne-Marie's case, takes discipline, but it doesn't have to be hard. It's within the reach of all of us. Happiness is a choice, one that each of us can make—and Anne-Marie Faiola shows us how.

—**Verne Harnish**, founder of Entrepreneurs' Organization (EO); founder and CEO of Gazelles; author of *Scaling Up*

WHY "BEST DAY EVER"?

Grinning through the grimaces and saying, "Best day ever!" whenever anyone ever asked me how my day was going has been a habit for more than a decade. It first started when I met my husband Chris. In the morning, when we were both fresh out of bed and still stumbling around, pre-coffee, making small talk, I'd often ask him how he'd slept or how he was feeling. He would frequently reply: "Happiness is a choice!" With the idea that we could choose our mind-set, I started actively choosing mine so that every day was the Best Day Ever. I hope this book helps you figure out how to make your day the Best Day Ever (and every day after that).

BESTDAYEVER.COM

This book, based on my own experiences, research, mentoring relationships, and insights from some of the world's most inspirational authors and speakers, is a collection of bite-size practical strategies you can start putting into practice today.

Each of the thirty-five strategies has exercises for you to read and work through. But please note: Whether you read the book in one sitting (wow!), complete the exercises while you're reading, or work through the book one strategy and one exercise at a time, there's no single "right way" to read this book.

I've divided these strategies into four categories:

1. *Be Responsible for Your Own Success!* You don't have to depend on "luck" when there are specific things you can

do to achieve new levels of success, both professionally and personally.

2. *Take Charge of Your Life!* Having a specific, carefully thought-out plan for your life will empower you and give you joy.

3. *Manage Your Resources!* Using time, money, and physical and personal strengths effectively is the foundation of success.

4. *You're in Control!* Don't give away your power; claim it and use it.

Even if you apply only one of the strategies in each of these four categories, it will bring a new level of everyday success into your life.

PART I

Be Responsible for Your Own Success!

Stop relying on "luck."

WRITE YOUR OWN STORY

Reframe your history to create
hope and meaning.

The most beautiful people we have known

are those who have known defeat,

known suffering, known struggle,

known loss, and have found their way out of the depths.

These persons have an appreciation,

a sensitivity, and an understanding of life

that fills them with compassions, gentleness,

and a deep loving concern.

Beautiful people do not just happen.

—ELIZABETH KUBLER-ROSS

Imagine a woman whose seven-year marriage has just broken up because her husband was sleeping with her best friend. Because she comes from a very religious family background, she feels a terrible sense of shame that her marriage has failed. She can't help but ask herself what she did wrong.

Then this woman, who just lost both her husband and her best friend, loses even more. Because of the divorce laws in her state, her ex-husband gets their house and every bit of her cash. She's left with nothing, just a bag of clothes, the silverware, and a painting her husband never liked. Although she does own a start-up business, she doesn't have even enough money to rent an apartment. The woman ends up sleeping on a friend's sofa because she has nowhere else to go. Then, on top of everything else, she gets physically sick.

Now imagine that two writers have been given the same assignment: to write a story about what happens next to this woman.

The first writer's story goes like this:

The woman sinks into depression. Everything in her life has fallen apart, so she reaches for whatever comfort she can find. She eats more junk food, and she drinks more alcohol. She's tired all the time, and she just doesn't have the energy to put into her business that she once did. Some days, she lies on the sofa watching television all day, too tired and sick to make herself get up and go to work. The business starts to go downhill, but she can't pull herself together enough to figure out what's wrong. She's just too sad, too tired, too sick.

When she meets a man who makes her feel good, she's so relieved to have some happiness in her life that she moves in with him right away. After a few months, though, she catches the man with another woman. Now she's even more depressed than she was before. "What is wrong with me?" she asks herself. "Why do these things keep happening to me?"

As the years go by, she sinks lower and lower. Her business fails. She has a series of relationships with men, but they all end with heartache. Physically and emotionally, she's constantly exhausted, prone to illnesses and upsets.

When she gets together with friends, they all complain endlessly about the no-good men in their lives and the jobs they hate, but her story is the saddest of them all. "You just have the worst luck," her friends tell her.

She nods, and her eyes fill with tears. "The day my husband betrayed me was the worst day ever," the woman tells her friends, "and every day since then has been just a little bit worse." As the story closes, the tears roll out of the woman's eyes. Her life is a tragedy.

The other writer's story is very different. It goes like this:

Sad, sick, and lonely, the woman forces herself to sit down and take a look at the goals she had in her life before everything fell apart. Her marriage is gone, but she still has her business. She makes up her mind to just keep putting one foot in front of the other toward her business goals. She's depressed, exhausted, angry, guilty, scared—but she gets up every morning and does what she has to do to keep her business on track. No matter how sick she feels, she doesn't miss a single day of work.

Deep in her heart, she still feels like a failure, but she knows that feelings don't always represent reality. She starts going to therapy once a week, getting the help she needs to cope with her emotions. Therapy is expensive, of course, and this means she's stuck sleeping on her friend's sofa that much longer. She's going to do whatever she has to do, though, to keep herself going, putting one foot in front of another in a slow trudge forward. Meanwhile, she's lonely, and she longs for another relationship with a man—but she's watched girl-friends go through bad breakups and then go out with other men just like the ones who broke their hearts the first time. She's not going to make that mistake.

Instead, one building block at a time, she's gradually rebuilding her life. She chooses friends who surround her with love and positive encouragement. She reads self-help books that teach her from a variety of perspectives—life coaching, Judeo-Christian, Buddhist—and she puts them all together with her own experiences to create a system of living that works for her.

Her business is growing now. She meets a man with whom she builds a stable, loving marriage, and they raise a family. Hard things happen to them, the way things always do, but so do wonderful things. The woman's life is rich and full of joy.

"You are so lucky," people frequently say to her, but she shakes her head. It's not luck that got her where she is today. Her life is a success story because she figured out what she needed to do to make it one.

As the second writer's story closes, the woman looks at her life and says, "Today is my best day ever." Then she smiles and adds, "And so was yesterday—and tomorrow will be too."

Every day is the woman's best day ever.

Both of these stories *could* have happened—but that second story is what actually *did* happen. I know, because it's my story. It's the one I chose for myself back when I was twenty-seven years old and my life fell apart.

There's nothing unique about my story. We all have our share of heartbreaks, but—as painful as they are—these awful disappointments are usually what teach us life's most valuable lessons. At least that's how it's worked in my life.

In the years since my divorce, I've had new triumphs as well as new failures, and along the way, through trial and error, I've learned some techniques for creating a successful life, both personally and as a businesswoman (there's a lot of overlap between the two). I collected here the thirty-five strategies that have helped me most. You've probably run across a lot of these ideas already in the course of your life. None of them is magic, and I don't pretend to offer you the secret to everlasting happiness and bliss.

What I do know, though, is that the more knowledge we have, the more power and freedom we have. In this book, I'll share some knowledge with you that's based on all I've learned over the years—through experience, research, and insights from some of the world's wisest and most inspirational authors and speakers. I'm giving you a smorgasbord of practical strategies you can start putting into practice right now. There is no single "right way" to do these things. Instead, I've provided a set of tools, a buffet of ideas, from which you may choose those that resonate with your personality, your history, and your desired future. I hope they will empower you to create your own success story.

Remember, you have a choice about the story you tell yourself. These best-practice strategies can help you tell an ongoing story of success. Today can be your best day ever.

And so can tomorrow—and the next day, and the day after that . . .

BUSINESS APPLICATION

In *The Art of Possibility*, authors Rosamund Stone Zander and Benjamin Zander share an example of how the stories we shape also affect our ability to perceive business opportunities:

A shoe factory sends two marketing scouts to a region of Africa to study the prospects for expanding business. One sends back a telegram saying,

SITUATION HOPELESS STOP NO ONE WEARS SHOES.

The other writes back triumphantly,

GLORIOUS BUSINESS OPPORTUNITY STOP THEY HAVE NO SHOES.

To the marketing expert who sees no shoes, all the evidence points to hopelessness. To his colleague, the same conditions point to abundance and possibility. Each scout comes to the scene with his own perspective; each returns telling a different tale. Indeed, all of life comes to us in narrative form; it's a story we tell.

EXERCISES FOR YOUR HEART AND MIND

The end-of-chapter exercises in this book are meant to prompt reflection and to get you to put thoughts on paper. You can write the answers on the pages here or use a dedicated notebook or journal for your reflections. But don't skip the exercises; they are meant to help you on your way along the Best-Day-Ever path.

MAKE IT PERSONAL

- All of us have at least one pivotal chapter in our lives, a place where the story we chose to tell sent us in one direction or another. Can you identify a chapter like that in your life? What was the story you chose to tell at that point? (Write it out in as great a detail as you can.)

- If you could change that story, even a little, how would you rewrite it? If you were a Hollywood screenwriter who had to find the silver lining in the story, how would you rewrite it?

- Each day brings a new chance to tell your story. What is the story you want to begin telling yourself and living today? (Write it in as great a detail as you can—and then reread it often in the days to come.)

INSPIRATION

Helen Keller inspired countless people with the story she chose for her life. As a blind and deaf woman in the early twentieth century, her life could very easily have been a tragic story of a bright spirit dimmed and hidden from view forever. But that isn't Helen Keller's story.

She wrote in her autobiography that most people think that a "happy life" depends on physical pleasures and material possessions. For these people, telling a story of success and achievement depends on winning some visible goal that they've chosen as the criterion for happiness. "If happiness is to be so measured," Keller wrote, "I who cannot hear or see have every reason to sit in a corner with folded hands and weep." Keller went on to say that if she, with all her immense challenges, could tell a tale of happiness, if her "happiness is so deep that it is a faith, so thoughtful that it becomes a philosophy of life," then her story that bears witness to the power of optimism is one we could all share in. "One who is called afflicted," she wrote, "rises up with the gladness of conviction" to tell a story of the goodness of life.

#2

YOUR UNIQUE EXPERIENCES + YOUR PERSONAL PASSION = WHAT THE WORLD NEEDS

Love the circumstances of your life unconditionally.

*Where our deep gladness
and the world's deep hunger meet,
we hear a further call.*

—FREDERICK BUECHNER

When I was in high school, I had what I thought was a great idea for a business. I loved my pet Russian dwarf hamsters, and I was convinced other people would love them too. So I decided to breed them and sell beautiful little Russian dwarf hamsters to people all around Lewis County, Washington, where I lived. That may sound like the weirdest idea ever for a business, but it actually worked.

I had a lot to learn, of course. I had to think about the gestation cycles of the hamsters and figure out how to plan so I would end up with the number of hamsters I would need in a month or two. Thankfully, my dad is a doctor, and he helped me to develop a birth-control system for the hamsters so I could put them on a breeding cycle. The market in Lewis County for Russian dwarf hamsters is fairly small, and I didn't want to end up with more inventory than I could sell.

My after-school job at a newspaper meant that I could place classified ads for free. (Remember, this was before the days of Craigslist.) Then, when the orders came in—and they did!—I made deliveries in my little used white Ford hatchback all around Lewis County. And I actually earned money because it turned out people wanted to have Russian hamsters for pets. There was a demand for what I had to offer.

On my side, it worked out well. The hamsters were free, the food didn't cost a lot, and I could sell each hamster for ten to fifteen dollars. It was great spending money for a teenager. What's more, I was learning valuable lessons about running a business that I could use over and over throughout my life.

One thing I learned was the power of combining my passion with customer service. I loved my little hamsters, and I wanted to make sure they were happy with their owners, so I'd do a follow-up call or two to make sure the hamsters were doing okay in their new environments. This meant asking the people if they had any questions: Did they know how to feed their new pets? Did they have any concerns about hamster behaviors? Did they wonder what the best cage was to house the little creatures? Google was not around in the 1990s, so the information I had to offer was appreciated and valued. My customers not only liked my hamsters, but they also liked me. You can't ask for any better marketing than that!

This was my first taste of the way in which something you love can be combined with your circumstances to create an opportunity—and that in turn can lead to still more opportunities later on. It's a principle that started there and continued to snowball through my life. I'm still living things I learned during the Hamster Chapter of my life.

There were other important chapters in my teenage years. At the same time that I was delivering my hamsters around the county, I also made use of another passion of mine—music. I got a job as a piano player for a ballet studio, a gig that taught me still more valuable lessons that I'm still using today. Shifting in an instant from playing fast-paced music for a mazurka to something slow and flowy for a waltz taught me flexibility. If my fingers were too fast or too slow, or I was playing the wrong song altogether, I heard about it from the teacher and the dancers. This meant I also learned very quickly how to take criticism without letting it destroy me.

These chapters of my life may have seemed trivial at the time, but looking back on them, I can see the value they offered. Even my darker chapters have helped illuminate my way and get me to where I am today. When I was young, for example, a random stranger tried to kidnap me while I was jogging in Lewis County, Washington. I first hid from him under a tree on a golf course and when I saw him opening the door to his van, ran for the safety of a nearby house, bursting in on a family watching TV. They took care of me while we waited for the police and my mom.

Because of those events, I wanted to go into criminal justice when I graduated from high school. Partly, I wanted to help people, but looking back, it's clear to me I also wanted to make myself feel safe. I wanted to be in control of my own life. I got my four-year degree in psychology and criminology because the almost-kidnapping had left me feeling out of control—and I was looking for a career that would allow me to impose order on all the scary chaos out there in the world.

I became a correctional officer, but working in the prison system wasn't at all what I had expected. It *was,* however, an eye-opening experience. I quickly realized that many of the people in the prison had never been given a chance in life. They had grown up without any good role models. They had been not only food insecure but also just plain starved half their lives. They had dads who were in prison. They had moms who were prostitutes. They had grandpas who injected them with heroin to keep them quiet during the day. They were abused by their uncles.

Encountering all this as a twenty-year-old, I felt as though I had been knocked over by a tsunami of hopelessness. I still wanted to help people, but my job at the prison seemed to accomplish too little to stem the enormous tide of despair. To help me cope with all that negative emotion, every night I would come home from work and make soap.

For some reason, making soap created a happy place for me where I could escape from the darkness I saw every day at work. It was a safe, predictable place where 2 + 2 = 4, because soapmaking is chemistry. It didn't have a bunch of complicated factors outside my control. So I made soap every single night. The sense of creativity it gave me was essential to my growing sense of happiness. Soon, though, I found myself with an excess of soap.

I could have looked at my job at the prison as a nonstarter, a misstep, something to be swept under the carpet of my memory. But, actually, it too was part of what got me where I am today. It triggered a new passion for handmade creativity—specifically, soapmaking.

You probably didn't have a hamster business when you were a teenager; you may not have ever worked in a prison, and I hope not very many of you experienced a kidnap attempt. Instead, you had a whole set of other wonderful, terrible, amazing experiences. One way or another, you've woven them into the story of your life, and that story has helped to shape who you are today.

All of us use our stories to create ourselves and our lives. Sometimes, though, we try to edit out a few chapters. We're conditioned to believe that if we can shape the events of our lives into a pretty story—or at least an interesting one—it has value; *that's* a story we want to claim and tell to the world. Meanwhile, we try to erase or forget the chapters that are embarrassing or sad or just plain boring.

But we wouldn't be who we are today without *all* the chapters of our lives. They're all important, in one way or another. Each chapter—including the silly ones, the boring ones, the sad ones, and even the embarrassing ones—can be transformed into gifts we give to ourselves and the world.

If you had asked me back when I was a teenager to predict what I would be doing when I grew up, I would never have guessed that I would build a successful business out of making soap. All those long-ago chapters—from hamsters to prisoners—led in a roundabout route to my present-day business that gives me so much joy and satisfaction. They were messy and not always pretty chapters, but they were *all* the early episodes for creating the Best Day Ever. I am happy with who I am today because I've claimed and integrated all these old chapters.

I didn't have some sort of extraordinary background that allowed me to succeed. Instead, I had stumbled upon a unique recipe that combined my passion with my life's circumstances—and it yielded things that the world needed and wanted.

You too have your own one-of-a-kind recipe to offer the world. It may not be hamsters or soap, and it may not be tangible goods at all—a tender heart, a generous spirit, or welcoming smile are all unique assets you can share. First, though, you must claim the stories of your life. Don't reject any of them.

Instead, love them all. This unconditional love is liberating. It lets you see the gifts your life has to offer you—and the world. What's more, love has a way of spreading throughout our lives— and living with love is a purposeful life, a life that leads to happiness and success.

 BUSINESS APPLICATION

Richard Branson, the Virgin Group founder, believes that the things that make us most excited about life are also the building blocks for good businesses. "When you believe in something," he says in an interview published on the Virgin website, "the force of your convictions will spark other people's interest and motivate them to help you achieve your goals. This is essential to success."

Branson also has advice if you find yourself on a path that no longer seems to connect with your personal story and passions. "Try to understand what motivated you to think in that direction in the first place," he says. "The passion behind your idea might lead you to the business or industry that you truly care about."

MAKE IT PERSONAL

Are there chapters in your life that you've overlooked or intentionally hidden out of sight? Let yourself go back in time to reexperience those chapters. Try to think of at least three and write them down. Don't discount any chapter as being too trivial, sad, or embarrassing to be worthy of your attention.

Now jot down a second list of things you learned during the course of each of those chapters. Maybe you learned to laugh at yourself. Or maybe your constant fights with your siblings taught you a lot about conflict resolution. Welcome and love each chapter—even those that seemed like failures at the time—and then circle the greatest gift each chapter brought to you.

Now, look at your two lists—and match up things you know how to do (thanks to your past experiences) or the things that benefit your life today with the lessons you gained from past experiences. Don't discount any possibilities. Be creative. Sometimes the wildest combination of ingredients yields the best result—and it may be the very thing that the world truly needs right now!

What passions do you have today that can be traced back to lessons learned from past less-than-wonderful experiences? Pick one or two combinations of passion and experience, and then think about ways to give that unique recipe expression in your life. It might be a business opportunity, it might be volunteer work, it might be a new hobby. Whatever it is, using it will enrich the world—and your life.

 INSPIRATION

In his book *Real Happiness: Proven Paths for Contentment, Peace & Well-Being,* Jonah Paquette retells an ancient Zen tale that illustrates the power we have to shape our perception of reality with the stories we tell about our lives. The story goes something like this:

Once a traveler made his way from a village in the mountains to a village in the valley. As he walked along, he saw a monk working in a field, so he stopped and asked, "Can you tell me what the village in the valley is like?"

The monk looked up from his work and instead of answering the traveler's question, he asked, "Where did you come from?"

"I have just come from the village in the mountains," the man said.

"What was that like?" the monk asked.

"Terrible! Everyone stared at me. No one spoke my language. I had to sleep on a dirt floor. The food was awful. My time there was one of the worst experiences of my life."

"Well," said the monk, "I'm afraid you will find the village in the valley is much the same."

A few hours later another traveler passed by the monk and said, "I am on my way to the village in the valley. Can you tell me what it's like?"

"Where have you come from?" the monk asked him.

"I have just come from the village in the mountains," the traveler said.

"And what was that like?" the monk asked.

"Amazing!" the man replied, "Everyone was interested in me, even though I was a stranger. We didn't speak the same language, so we had to communicate using our hands and expressions. We ended up laughing and laughing together. One family welcomed me into their home, even though they were so poor that the only place to sleep was on the dirt floor. They shared their dinner with me, so I had the chance to try new foods I'd never eaten before. What an adventure! And what kind people! Being with them was one of the best experiences of my life."

"Then," said the monk, "I think you will find that the village in the valley is much the same."

#3

YOU CAN'T DIVORCE SUCCESS FROM DISCIPLINE

Discipline is what makes success look easy.

We must all suffer from one of two pains:
the pain of discipline or the pain of regret.

—JIM ROHN

Do you ever look at someone else's life and think, "She's so lucky—but I could never be her"? Or maybe you think, "Success comes so easily to her. I feel like a failure by comparison." Thoughts like that are feeding into a storyline you don't have to live.

Success isn't some amazing good luck people stumble across. It doesn't just happen, and it's often not the result of some special skill or ability. But success requires something important, something that's available to you too—discipline.

If you happen to be a working parent, your mornings are probably filled with the pandemonium of childcare, cajoling, spilled coffee, and mad dashes to school drop-off. Mine are like that, too. Then, I spend a full day at work doing whatever it takes to support my team, lead the company, and make a difference: everything from teaching people how to make soap live on the Bramble Berry Facebook page, to working on a new challenge for Best Day Ever, to human resources decisions. Like most busy people, I find that the day goes by in a blur. Often, lunch is eaten quickly at my desk between phone calls and typing so I can fit in a much-needed daily workout during the regular lunch break. Once home, it is utter and complete chaos, usually with a side of laughter, as any parent to toddlers can attest. After the kids are finally in bed, there's precious little time to finish up work for the day, connect with my husband, and read a book before falling asleep, usually with the book in my lap. The next morning, the whole cycle starts again.

You might think all this could make me feel stressed and overwhelmed. Well, yes, some days it does! A perfect balance of all the factors in life is simply impossible to achieve. Although I know the truth of that fact, it's still a struggle at times not to tell myself, "My life is just too much. I'll never pull off everything I have to do. *I just can't.*" Those are the days when I have to remind myself that I have the freedom to choose to live a different story. To do that, I *choose* to activate daily discipline.

"Willpower" is often used as another word for the kind of discipline I'm talking about. Psychologists define it as the ability to "delay gratification"—in other words, you do something you don't want to do now, so that you can get something you want later on.

According to an American Psychological Association survey, the number-one reason people give for not making healthy lifestyle changes is: "I don't have enough willpower." People talk about

Anywhere you see this icon in the margin, you'll be able to find more information in the Further Reading and Viewing List *on page 345.*

willpower as though it were something similar to a musical talent or the ability to curl your tongue—you're either born with it or you're not. If you don't have it, oh well, too bad.

It turns out, though, that willpower is a little like a muscle: the more you use it, the stronger it gets. Like a muscle, though, it can also get exhausted, so you need to take care of it. It uses a part of your brain, scientists say, that must be replenished the same way the rest of your body is—with sleep and healthy foods (which we'll be covering in Strategy #23). When you have to use all your powers of self-discipline in one particular area of your life over a long period of time, you may find it harder to control yourself in other areas of your life. For example, in one study, people who were asked to control their emotions were more likely to spend money on unnecessary items, whereas others who were told to resist sweets tended to procrastinate more.

Scientists have also found that certain activities can drain a person's willpower—such as sitting through a boring meeting while resisting the urge to fidget or doodle or yawn. According to some researchers, resisting the urge to check our phones, e-mail, or social media accounts is another constant factor that depletes modern-day willpower. The human brain was not set up to deal with all the immediate gratification that's offered online these days.

The good news, though, is that researchers have found tricks that can help us strengthen our willpower. Here are a few I've come across that (usually) work for me:

- ***Find something that puts you in a good mood.*** In a recent study, scientists asked a group of people to use up their willpower by resisting a particular temptation. After that, half the group received unexpected gifts or watched a funny video (things likely to put them in a good mood).

The other half of the group simply rested during the same period of time. Compared to people who just rested for a brief period, those whose moods were improved did significantly better in resisting another set of temptations.

- **Clench your muscles.** Studies say that exercising control over any body part causes you to become more disciplined in other facets of life. You could clench your fist, squeeze your eyes shut, or tighten your calf muscles.

- **Meditate.** We all know that meditation is great for a lot of things (like managing stress and increasing mental focus), but some recent research indicates that even a short period of meditation can help build willpower.

- **Don't let yourself get hungry.** When we're hungry, our blood sugar drops, and when our blood sugar levels are low, scientists have found that we have less willpower. Don't just grab a candy bar, though, which will make your blood sugar spike and then plummet. You need to eat the right kinds of food—plenty of protein, complex carbohydrates, and healthy fats—to keep your blood sugar steady.

John Pierpont said, "The first step towards getting somewhere is to decide you're not going to stay where you are." Back when my first marriage failed, I was determined that I wasn't going to stay stuck where I was. It took some hard-to-muster discipline to choose to tell myself a success story rather than a tragedy—and it takes discipline every single day for me to get out of bed and do all the things that need doing in my busy day.

That's one of the features of discipline: It's something you do over and over, day after day. You slip up some days. And then you get right back to it the next day and the day after that, month after month, year after year. You can't choose a Best-Day-Ever storyline without lots and lots of discipline, deciding morning after morning the story you want to live that day.

BUSINESS APPLICATION

Self-discipline is essential to entrepreneurial success. Research studies (see the reading list at the back of the book) have found a couple of strategies for increasing your workday willpower:

1. Many businesspeople have tapped into the power of early mornings to build productivity and effectiveness. Even if you don't think of yourself as a "morning person," mornings may be the best time to devote yourself to the jobs you find least attractive. Researchers have found that most people have more willpower early in the day, so it's a good time to tackle things you tend to procrastinate doing. Later in the day, after you've been dealing with people, making decisions, and focusing on countless tasks, your "willpower muscles" become depleted. By getting important things done early in the day, you will have more willpower to get more done, increasing your professional productivity.

2. Listen to music during the afternoon while you're at work. Music replenishes the "willpower muscles" in your brain, making it easier for you to stick to your goals throughout the day.

Several studies have found that willpower—or self-discipline—has more influence on long-term business success than does intelligence.

MAKE IT PERSONAL

- On a scale of 1 to 10 (1 being next to nothing, and 10 being lots and lots), how would you rate yourself when it comes to how much discipline (or willpower) you have?

- Are there some areas of your life where you would rate yourself higher in terms of discipline? (For example, maybe you're good at exercising but not so good at saying no to junk food. Or you're terrible at turning the television off at night, but you jump out of bed every morning for your meditation time.) Make a list under two headings labeled "Discipline Successes" and "Discipline Challenges."

- Now look at these two lists and ask yourself: Why is discipline easier in some situations than in others? What makes the difference?

- Now ask yourself: Can I use these insights to move at least one item from the "challenges" column into the "successes" column? If so, which ones and why?

- Next, take some time to think about this: Is a physical reason—tiredness, lack of sleep, or poor diet, for example—making it harder for you to have willpower in certain situations? Which items in your "challenges" list might become easier if you made certain changes in your lifestyle—and what would those changes be?

- Over the next month, practice using discipline to tackle at least one item on your "challenges" list. Write down which behavior you are going to address with willpower. Describe the changes you will make in your life to help you do so. Notice if it becomes easier or harder as the days go by. (You should expect it to become harder before it becomes easier. Like all muscles, the willpower muscle "hurts" when you first start to exercise it!)

 INSPIRATION

Kieran Behan is an Irish gymnast who would never have been able to compete in the Olympics without discipline. He started gymnastics young, but when he was ten years old, he had a tumor removed from his thigh that doctors told him would prevent him from ever walking again, much less competing as a gymnast.

"That just drove me on," Kieran told the *New York Times* in 2012. "I wanted to prove them wrong. They were saying it was over but I wasn't having it." In other words, Kieran refused to believe the story the doctors were telling him. Instead, he chose a different story to live.

Kieran tackled the grueling exercises that helped him regain mobility, and after a year, he was able to walk again. By the time he was fourteen, he was once more practicing gymnastics. Then he ran into yet another roadblock to his dream of become a gymnast: he hit his head on the high bar during practice, seriously injuring his brain. This time he lost not only his ability to perform but also the ability to talk and feed himself.

And once again, Kieran surprised his doctors by getting back on his feet—and back on the bars. He was disciplined about his training, and he kept at it, even when he had to sweep the gym floors to pay for his lessons.

Finally, his discipline got him where he had wanted to go: He qualified for his first European Championships in 2010—only to suffer yet another setback when he tore a ligament in his knee. "It was the nearest I ever came to quitting," he admitted. "Sheer despair, really, but I'd been through a lot worse and knew that, whatever happened, I could always come back."

His inner discipline allowed him to bounce back to win three World Cup medals in 2011. His dream had finally come true. "I felt like I was in a fairy tale when I got here," he said. Years of discipline had paid off—and now he was making success look easy. He continued to train and compete at the top levels for his sport, representing Ireland at the 2016 Olympics in Brazil.

SUCCESS CAN BE SYSTEMATIZED

Replicate small victories every day.

Success is neither magical nor mysterious.
Success is the natural consequence
of consistently applying basic fundamentals.

—JIM ROHN

As we just said in Strategy #3, success depends on discipline. But I can hear some of you saying, "I'm one of those people with no willpower. I just don't have it in me to be disciplined. My life is too busy. I'm too tired. I'm too depressed. I'm too heavy or too sick or too poor or too whatever."

Great news—whatever you're telling yourself probably isn't true. You're *not* too anything to make small changes—and small changes accumulate into big changes when compounded with the magic of time. Discipline comes a lot easier when you apply it to smaller pieces of your life.

Don't ask discipline to do the heavy lifting required to achieve goals like, "I will lose fifty pounds," or, "I will change my ho-hum marriage into a happy, satisfying relationship." Instead, take a look at those big goals and figure out how you could break them down into tiny, daily, achievable tasks. Those mini-goals are how you systematize success.

One of the good things about bite-size goals is that you can easily measure them. For example, one of my daily goals is "compliment my husband at least once." Over time, this leads to him feeling consistently appreciated within our relationship, a good thing in any marriage. For this goal, measuring success is a yes or no answer. Did I do it or did I not? This goal is small and doesn't seem overwhelming to do daily.

A seemingly trivial goal I set for myself six years ago was to improve my gum health. I systematized this by committing to flossing every single day. I told everyone that I was going to floss every day; I put it on my blog, and every day I checked off a simple yes or no. The daily goal was so tiny—it takes about a minute to floss your teeth—that I didn't feel discouraged every time I thought about doing it. And the more yeses I could check off, the better I felt about myself. Those small, daily victories gave me momentum to keep going. And now, six years later, I still floss every day. As the years went by, my dentist at first was measuring my gum health at 3 on a scale of 0 to 5 for periodontal decay, then I was down to 2, then 1, and at my last visit, I was at 0. That's success one little "yes" at a time!

The same principle of small, systematized, daily successes can be applied to far grander goals too. Do you want to get in shape? Then instead of taking on a rigorous exercise program, maybe you commit to simply moving your body, in one way or another, for twenty minutes every single day, no excuses. Do you want to improve your health? Something as small as drinking eight glasses of water every day could make a real difference in your overall physical well-being. So could going to bed a half hour earlier. Do you want to learn a new language? After spending just fifteen minutes a day practicing for one year, you could find yourself surprisingly fluent. Or if you sent your husband a card once a week telling him how much you loved him and how proud of him you were for one specific thing (different each week), how might that change your relationship after fifty-two weeks?

Another good thing about systematizing success is that eventually those tiny daily victories turn into habit. I no longer have to remind myself to floss my teeth, because it's a habit—and habits don't take nearly as much energy and effort as willpower. Willpower is white-knuckling it. Habits, however, create ruts that become easier and easier to follow the more you use them.

Think about it. I bet you don't have to decide whether to brush your teeth every morning. It's not a big argument you have to have with yourself every day to make yourself squeeze that tube of toothpaste. You just do it because it's habit. There's very little energy required to maintain basic dental hygiene.

Habits can also be destructive, of course. But why not take advantage of the positive power of habit? Systematize your success into small victories you achieve each and every day, and you will find discipline will come far more easily. Your best day ever will be within your reach—every day.

BUSINESS APPLICATION

Researchers Teresa Amabile and Steven J. Kramer have found what they call the "progress principle"—in other words, the power of small wins to move businesses forward. In a 2011 *Harvard Business Review* article, they write, "Through exhaustive analysis of diaries kept by knowledge workers, we discovered the progress principle: Of all the things that can boost emotions, motivation, and perceptions during a workday, the single most important is making progress in meaningful work. And the more frequently people experience that sense of progress, the more likely they are to be creatively productive in the long run. Whether they are trying to solve a major scientific mystery or simply produce a high-quality product or service, everyday progress—even a small win—can make all the difference in how they feel and perform."

The progress principle isn't only something that entrepreneurs should apply to their own lives, say Amabile and Kramer; they should also use this principle to make their entire businesses more effective. "To become an effective manager," they write, "you must learn to set this positive feedback loop in motion. That may require a significant shift. Business schools, business books, and managers themselves usually focus on managing organizations or people. But if you focus on managing progress, the management of people—and even of entire organizations—becomes much more feasible. You won't have to figure out how to x-ray the inner work lives of subordinates; if you facilitate their steady progress in meaningful work, make that progress salient to them, and treat them well, they will experience the emotions, motivations, and perceptions necessary for great performance. Their superior work will contribute to organizational success. And here's the beauty of it: They will love their jobs."

 MAKE IT PERSONAL

- What is a BIG goal you'd like to achieve?

- Now think about small daily tasks that will help you get closer to that goal. List at least three that you can commit to doing daily over the next month.

- Measure your success with these goals by placing a checkmark next to one, each day that you achieve it. After a month, how many checkmarks do you have? Are you finding these small tasks easier to do yet? Can you commit to these tasks for another month—or six months? A classic mental trick to get you past the brain's natural desire to shrug off new habits is to promise yourself a reward at the end of the time period with certain performance. For example, my goal is to be 85 percent sugar-free this year. If I make that goal, I will splurge on the latest, greatest smartwatch. That adds extra motivation for me to push past and through those longer time periods of three or six months.

 INSPIRATION

Books—the right books—can help us reach Best-Day-Ever success. A book you may find helpful as you think about systematizing success is *The Power of Habit: Why We Do What We Do in Life and Business* by Charles Duhigg. Here are some quotes from the book:

"Typically, people who exercise start eating better and becoming more productive at work. They smoke less and show more patience with colleagues and family. They use their credit cards less frequently and say they feel less stressed. Exercise is a keystone habit that triggers widespread change."

"Champions don't do extraordinary things. They do ordinary things, but they do them without thinking, too fast for the other team to react. They follow the habits they've learned."

"Small wins are exactly what they sound like, and are part of how keystone habits create widespread changes. A huge body of research has shown that small wins have enormous power, an influence disproportionate to the accomplishments of the

victories themselves . . . . Once a small win has been accomplished, forces are set in motion that favor another small win. Small wins fuel transformative changes by leveraging tiny advantages into patterns that convince people that bigger achievements are within reach."

#5

FEET FIRST,
NOT HEAD FIRST

Small starts can lead to great success.

Do not be afraid of a small beginning.
Great things come afterwards.

—SWAMI VIVEKANANDA

After nine months as a correctional officer, I couldn't stand it anymore. All I wanted to do was make soap. My ex-husband, whom I was putting through school at the time, said to me, "I'll tell you what—you can have three months to do this fun little hobby of yours. If you can make money in three months, we'll consider you starting a business." Thinking back, I can hear how patronizing that sounded, but at the time, I was just excited. I quit my job and started selling soap on the weekends.

My first weekend—at the Mount Vernon Tulip Festival—I sold a thousand dollars' worth of soap. I was thrilled, amazed, inspired. It was a huge light-bulb moment, where suddenly everything seemed to come together and make sense.

As a correctional officer, part of my responsibility had been trying to line up jobs for people after they were released. The goal was to keep people from ending up back in prison, but my work hadn't given me much hope for the system. Now, however, I was thinking, "How many people are out there who could make money from soap the way I am? I wonder if I can help them. Can I teach them how to make soap while I sell soap on the weekends?" My work in the prison had never seemed as though it accomplished much when it came to helping people. But soapmaking? "Oh my gosh!" I thought. "This is the way I can *really* help people. I can give them knowledge that will give them greater power and freedom. I can do this!" I was inspired.

I maxed out my credit card, put up a Microsoft Word document website, and started selling soap on the weekends while teaching people how to make soap during the week and selling them the ingredients. My weekday occupation turned into Bramble Berry, my business today that sells ingredients to soapmakers all over the world. I sold soap every weekend for five years, while I was building Bramble Berry during the week.

Life wasn't easy. I worked at Bramble Berry every weekday, then I'd come home and make soap and label soap at night. Every Saturday morning, I loaded up my little Subaru hatchback, strapped my display to the top, and drove to the craft show or farmers' market where I set up my booth and sold soap from ten in the morning until six or seven at night. Saturday nights, I often slept in my car, because I couldn't afford a hotel. Sunday morning, I'd do it all again, then load up everything in my car, drive back home, and do my Bramble Berry work . . . until the next weekend, when I'd be off to another craft fair or farmers' market. Ever so slowly—painfully—year by year, Bramble Berry grew into the successful business it is today.

I'm not saying, though, that you should quit your job and launch headlong into whatever *your* passion is. Too often you hear people say, "Follow your passion," as though passion alone is all you need to find success. You don't have to dive headfirst into the deep end of the pool and then discover you don't know how to swim nearly as well as you thought you did. Instead, you can step into the shallow end, and then make your way deeper and deeper, one step at a time.

In my case, this meant I worked hard on the weekends to keep a steady income stream that would support myself and my husband, while at the same time I worked on growing Bramble Berry. I didn't dive in over my head before I knew if I could swim. I kept my financial safety net in place—selling soap on the weekends—until I was certain Bramble Berry could support me.

Following your passion is a great thing—but it doesn't necessarily mean you'll make a ton of money doing whatever it is. In fact, odds are good that at the beginning you won't make much at all. So start out small. Try a little something. Does it make money? If yes, great! Do it some more. Expand a little. If the answer is no, though, then you haven't lost more than you can afford to lose. Now it's time to rethink your approach. Try something slightly different.

And then go just a little deeper into the pool.

 ## BUSINESS APPLICATION

When we look at the world's most famous businesses, it's easy to forget that they came from small beginnings. The founders of companies like Amazon, Apple, and Google didn't start out trying to create these businesses as they exist today. Instead, they started by creating something much smaller—an online bookstore, a computer, and a search algorithm.

They also didn't start out by going deep in debt to buy a fancy, impressive building for their new venture. They used the resources they had. Start-ups that began in garages are famous. Here are five businesses that began in a garage—and grew:

1. **Amazon**: When Jeff Bezos founded Amazon. com in 1994, it was completely run out of his garage in Bellevue, Washington. He didn't sell his first book until July 1995.

2. **Apple**: In 1976, Steve Jobs and Steve Wozniak started Apple Computers by hand-building fifty units of Wozniak's Apple I Computer in a garage.

3. **Disney**: Walt started his career filming the Alice Comedies in his uncle's garage. The short films would eventually become part of the original *Alice's Wonderland*.

4. **Harley Davidson**: In 1901, twenty-one-year-old William S. Harley drew up plans to create a small engine to power a bicycle, and then for the next two years, he and his friend Arthur Davidson built their motor-bicycle in a ten-by-fifteen-foot shed (which was pretty much

like a garage—except that garages hadn't been invented yet).

5. **Hewlett-Packard**: In 1939, Bill Hewlett and Dave Packard founded HP in their garage with an initial investment of $538. Their first product was an audio oscillator and one of their first customers was Walt Disney, who purchased eight oscillators to develop the sound system for the movie *Fantasia*.

 MAKE IT PERSONAL

- If money were not an issue, what passion would you put out into the world?

- Now think about a way you can start this passion feet first rather than head first. What could you try out in the very near future? How much do you stand to lose if it flops? Is that an acceptable loss?

- "Passion play" is something you do on the side or in your free time for fun and renewal because it inspires you and you're passionate about it. It could be a hobby (knitting), it could be volunteer work (eldercare), or it could be a side business (healthy ketogenic cookies that ship all over the United States). What will your passion play be?

INSPIRATION

When Philip Glass was a child, his father diversified his job as a radio repairman by stocking records. Then he brought home the records that didn't sell so he could listen to them and figure out why people weren't buying them—and this was when Philip was first exposed to a rich array of music, from bebop to hillbilly, as well as works by more offbeat composers.

When Philip grew up, music was his passion—but he made his living as a plumber and taxi driver. Even when his musical work was finally premiering at the Met, he was still doing plumbing, and he renewed his taxi license, just in case.

In an interview with the *Guardian* in 2001, he said that one time while he was working as a plumber, "I suddenly heard a noise and looked up to find Robert Hughes, the art critic of *Time* magazine, staring at me in disbelief. 'But you're Philip Glass! What are you doing here?' It was obvious I was installing his dishwasher, and I told him I would soon be finished. 'But you are an artist,' he protested. I explained that I was an artist but that I was sometimes a plumber as well and that he could go away and let me finish."

Philip Glass—who has written operas, musical theatre works, ten symphonies, eleven concertos, sonatas, and film scores—didn't earn a living from making music until he was forty-two!

Today, Philip Glass is one of the most influential modern-day music makers. He followed his passion in small steps all the way to greatness.

Great things happen when small steps are compounded by the power of time.

Success is easy if you think of it like rust.
It's inevitable if you keep at it.

— FRED FRANZIA

On Friday, March 13, 2015, the boiler that heated our house mysteriously and randomly exploded. In the process, it took out walls, ripped out natural gas lines, and ruined the furniture and belongings in multiple rooms. Seven fire trucks and forty-two firemen responded to the emergency. It was a disaster.

My husband, Chris, and I had a one-year-old and a three-year-old, two jobs to manage—and no house to live in. During the months after the explosion, we had to move five times while coping with all the insane demands of our life. Fortunately, we gradually got past that crazy chapter of our lives, the kids stayed healthy, and (rather amazingly) neither my husband nor I missed a single day of work.

My husband isn't Superman, and I'm certainly not Superwoman. If we had stopped to think about the immense challenges we faced, then we would have been overwhelmed. The only way we coped was by breaking down the craziness into smaller, manageable tasks, and then divvying them up between us. We made a master list of everything that needed to be done, and we passed it back and forth to each other. Since our house was cordoned off during the investigation, we couldn't get to our closets, so someone had to buy clothes for all of us to wear. Someone had to deal with the insurance company. Someone had to figure out how to get into the house to get the keys for our other car. Someone had to meet the inspectors at the house. Someone had to meet with the people at the bank to get a loan to bridge the gap until the insurance money came in. If Chris had a less-busy week, he was the one meeting all the contractors at the house, and I was the one doubling down at work. When he was busy at work, I took care of the insurance details. Ultimately, by taking one slow step at a time, we both got through it with our sanity and our marriage intact—and we ended up in a house we like even more than the one we lost.

Most of us like to think of life in terms of great adventures and amazing achievements but, many times, success is simply the product of doing the same thing—the same tactic, the same practice, the same exercise, the same tedious little task—over and over, day after day. It sounds boring, but it's also comforting when you're in the middle of a crisis or during those times when life seems overwhelming. Believing in the power of the slow trudge can get you over even the steepest challenges. I've learned that from experience. The slow trudge was the only way we got through that period when we had to rebuild a home.

The power of the trudge can do amazing things in *your* life, too. For example, if you want to have physical health, then you're not going to run a marathon one weekend and then sit on the couch the rest of the year. Instead, you'll need to move every day. If you want to have a company that has fantastic customer service, then you can't sit down and answer all your customer e-mails in one day once a year; you have to answer them every single day. Great things happen when you do small steps that are compounded by the power of time.

This approach will get you through the crises in your life, but it's also great for when you want to improve your life in a variety of ways. Your job may seem so challenging and exhausting that when you come home all you want to do is slump down on the sofa and watch TV—but small steps don't require that much energy. By doing one or two small things every day, you can transform your life.

Last year, for example, when I went back to school for my nutritional therapy certification, the baby steps toward that goal consisted of studying at least twenty minutes a day. Twenty minutes a day was the litmus test for success or failure. Many days, I studied more than twenty minutes, but so long as I was consistent about at least those twenty minutes, I knew I would ultimately reach my goal.

Consistency is powerful. Pulling a last-minute all-nighter might have worked for us in college, when we tried to cram an entire semester of studying into a single night, but it doesn't work out in the grown-up world—not if we want to achieve something that's truly worthwhile. Best-Day-Ever success comes from all those tiny consistent steps, one after another, when you're tired, when you're bored, when you're sad, no matter what.

At first those big self-improvement goals—"I'm going to quit smoking," "I'm going to lose fifty pounds," "I'm going to start a new career"—can seem exciting. You feel energized by the sheer enormity of what you hope to accomplish. Pretty soon, though, the enormity will feel daunting. You'll get tired and slip up. Then you'll slip up again, and this time you'll find yourself resenting that big goal. The third time you slip up, you'll be saying, "That was a stupid goal anyway. I don't want to bother with it anymore."

Let's say you want to quit sugar. Rather than saying, "I'm quitting all sugar, including honey," you could say, "I'm not going to have regular sugar in my coffee. I'm going to downgrade to honey, and I will not eat refined sugar in the form of candy." That's your goal. That's it. Do that for a month. Do it for six months. Then do it for a year. By that time, it will have become a habit and you can set yourself a new, slightly more challenging goal if you want. You'll be healthier than if you had done nothing—and you are far more likely to be consistent about small, manageable goals than if you had set yourself an impossibly high mountain to climb.

On his website, author James Clear shares a simple yet powerful strategy for utilizing the power of the trudge. In 1993, twenty-three-year-old Trent Dyrsmid was a rookie stockbroker who surprised everyone by making immediate progress toward success, thanks to two jars and some paper clips. Every day he would start with 120 paper clips in one jar, while the other jar was empty. At eight o'clock in the morning, he started making calls, and each time he made a phone call, he would move a paper clip from the full jar to the empty jar. For the rest of the day, he just kept making calls until all the paper clips had been moved from one jar to the other. After a year and a half of making 120 calls every day, his book of business grew to $5 million in assets. Within a few years, other firms were recruiting him because of his success, and eventually he got a new job where he was making $200,000 a year. Trent earned his success one paper clip at a time. The paper clips gave him a visual cue that helped him to commit to the same small act over and over and over, day after day.

Consider using the paper clip strategy to motivate you for the slow trudge. And remember—even though the trudge can get boring, it's also hopeful. Just do this one small thing, every day, and it will change your life.

MAKE IT PERSONAL

- What are two ways you would like to improve your life? These are things that affect your day-to-day existence (not the same as your BIG goal from Strategy #4).

- Now make a list of one, two, or three small things that will get you closer to each of those improvements. Remember to keep them small enough and easy enough that you'll be able to do them every single day. Example: If your improvement goal is weight loss or more energy, the measurable daily trudge could be to start every morning with a lemon water or to be in bed by 10:30 p.m. daily.

#6

USE A LONG-TERM PERSPECTIVE

Everything you do has countless reverberations.

Everything in your life is a reflection of a choice you have made.
If you want a different result, make a different choice.

—UNKNOWN

Imagine that, as you're rushing to get ready for your day, you notice your spouse has forgotten to do something you'd asked him to do. You're in a hurry and already feeling impatient, so you snap at him. He snaps back, and you spend the next five minutes squabbling over nothing.

When you get to work, you're still thinking about how angry you are. Instead of focusing on whatever would be the most productive thing for you to be doing, you spend the next twenty minutes staring at your computer screen and thinking about that tiny irritation that grew into a squabble.

Those twenty nonproductive minutes put you a little behind in your work—and that makes you feel a little more irritable than you were before. When a coworker says something that sounds to you like a criticism, you take offense. Later in the day, you notice that another colleague made a mistake that will take some time to fix, and you lose your temper. She points out that you're behind in your work, and the two of you argue.

Your entire day is filled with small defeats. By the time you drive home, you're so crabby that all you want to do is sit down with a glass of wine and some junk food. As you walk in your door, you tell your spouse, "I had a terrible day. Absolutely everything went wrong."

He grunts something, but you know he doesn't really care—he's still grouchy about the fight you had before work—and the two of you snipe at each other the rest of the evening. You're exhausted and upset, so you pour yourself a giant glass of wine and open a bag of potato chips. After the day you had, you deserve it!

Your day didn't have to have to be like that. Rewind the day and start over. You notice that your spouse forgot to do something that you asked him to do, and you open your mouth to snap at him. But then you catch yourself. The world really isn't going to end because he forgot to do whatever it is. You can remind him tonight after work.

The two of you kiss goodbye and say, "I love you"; you go to work with a warm glow inside as you think about how much you love your spouse. You're smiling as you start your workday, but your happiness doesn't interfere with your focus on what you need to do that day.

When a coworker sticks her head in the door with a complaint, the two of you are able to talk through the issue, and a new idea comes out of the conversation that will improve your work. Later in the day when you notice that another colleague has made a mistake, you take the time to understand what happened. After talking with her, you see how something you did contributed to her mistake, and the two of you are able to work through a solution that will prevent similar mistakes from happening in the future.

By the time you drive home from work, you're feeling a sense of achievement that you were able to accomplish so much. As you walk in the door, your spouse asks, "How was your day?"

"Wonderful!" you say. "I got so much done—and I had a couple of conversations that led to some real breakthroughs."

You think about pouring yourself a glass of wine, but you realize that going for a walk before dinner is what you'd rather do. Your spouse goes along, and as you walk, you're filled with a sense of contentment. "I had the best day," you say to him.

We've all had days like both of these. We tend to think it's just the luck of the draw—some days are good, some days are bad, some are a little of both. But guess what? Really, we have more control than we think.

"Live in the moment" is a popular saying—but living with that moment-by-moment awareness doesn't mean that we ignore the effect each instant has on the future. Instead, we recognize that even the smallest choices we make will reverberate into the future. Each moment matters.

It sounds like a contradiction, but living in the moment can also mean we take a long-term perspective on life. We recognize that each moment offers us a choice as to how we will respond. In the instant when we notice our loved ones forgot to do something, snapping at them might be the easiest response. It might even give us the most momentary satisfaction. After all, they deserve our anger, right? Except that tiny little choices like this have long-term effects.

We've all been there and have made the choice to lash out instead of swallowing a small irritation. It never ends well.

Long-term thinking pays off in many areas of life. If you look at the imaginary scenario that opened this chapter, there wasn't just one moment that sent its reverberations into the future; there were many. Each moment presented a choice. For example, at the end of that day, the choice of whether to drink a glass of wine or go for walk will impact how you feel in the future. There is a cumulative effective to decisions like these; the more times you opt for junk food and wine instead of going for a walk before dinner, the less overall energy you will have, and the greater the negative impact on your ongoing health. In a similar way, spending money on impulse buys can feel good in the moment, but it too has a cumulative long-term effect.

Here's a rule of thumb to remember: Long-term thinking is harder in the present moment, but it makes things easier down the road. Short-term thinking feels easy in the moment, but it makes your future life harder.

Thinking about the long-term reverberations of each tiny choice is a powerful life guide. As we've already described in earlier strategies, even the tiniest actions can get you closer to your big goals, and the discipline we talked about in Strategy #3 (You Can't Divorce Success from Discipline) manifests itself through this long-term thinking process. When you focus on your vision of the future— whether that's later in the day or a year from now—you boost your willpower to make better choices now.

 BUSINESS APPLICATION

Thinking long term is a key factor in any business or career. Often, though, we connect long-term business thinking with huge leaps forward—like when the founder of Soft Soap (the first popular liquid soap) purchased all the spring pumps in the entire world to force Colgate-Palmolive to purchase their small, upstart business—or Elon Musk's double-down on batteries as a way to control the electric car market—or even Steve Job's foresight in locking in the worldwide rights to the Toshiba flash drive to edge out any other players from entering the music-in-your-pocket market. Whether you agree with their aggressive tactics or not, these were big decisions that showcased planning, foresight, and long-term thinking.

Most of us recognize the big decisions we have made in our business lives and the impact those decisions had. We're aware that the times we decided to fire a manager, buy a new building, or expand into a new market had profound effects on our business. But we may not be as aware of the small decisions that we make that impact our lives every day—things like what we had for breakfast, whether we took time to chat with a colleague, or the tone of voice we used when talking to employees.

John Wooden writes, "There is a choice you have to make in everything you do. So keep in mind that in the end, the choice you make, makes you!" When we overlook the many small choices we make each day, we're not really seeing the big picture. We also need to remember that even choices we consider personal can have profound effects on our professional performance. Decisions having to do with diet, exercise, kindness, and integrity will all impact our businesses and careers—and sometimes small, overlooked choices can end up having large negative results we never anticipated.

 MAKE IT PERSONAL

- As you look back at the last few days, can you see a point at which a choice you made in the moment had negative long-term consequences? Describe that incident and how its reverberations have affected your life since then.

- How might you have reacted differently? Describe the other choices that were available to you. How do you think another choice might have affected your life?

- We are accustomed to reacting thoughtlessly to stimuli. This can make it difficult to form new habits. Think of a cue you can use to remind yourself that your choices have long-term consequences. It could be something as simple as thinking to yourself, "Long-term!" or "Breathe!" It might be wearing a piece of jewelry that represents your future goals and touching it whenever your short-term response could threaten that long-term perspective. You might even choose a song to sing (if only in your mind) that will give you time to think before you react. Take some time to think about what will work best for you. Then write it down and practice it over the next few days. If you practice this strategy long enough, then it will eventually become a habit that will strengthen your discipline and help you reach your future goals—one moment at a time.

 INSPIRATION

We often hear about "overnight success" stories— but almost always, when you learn the whole story, that apparently amazing and instant success was actually built on years of much smaller choices.

The Pokémon Go app is a good example of this. It had more than 10 million downloads in the first week after it was released, and people credited its creator, John Hanke, with a massive overnight craze. But that "overnight success" actually took twenty years to build. Here's how it went:

In 1996, while still a student, Hanke helped create the very first MMO (massively multiplayer online game) called Meridian 59. He sold the game to 3DO to move on to a bigger passion of his: mapping the world.

Then, in 2000, Hanke launched Keyhole, which linked maps with aerial photography, leading to the first online, GPS-linked 3D aerial map of the world.

In 2004, Google bought Keyhole, and with Hanke's help, turned Keyhole into what is now Google Earth.

From 2004 to 2010, Hanke focused on making GPS-based games, while at the same time, he created Google Maps and Google Street View. During this time, he also collected the team that would later create Pokémon Go.

In 2010, Hanke launched a start-up funded by Google called Niantic Labs to create a game layer on maps.

In 2012, Hanke created Niantic's first geo-based MMO, which he called "Ingress," where he layered online activity on top of the real world via smart-phones. Hanke said that this was something he used to daydream about during his daily commute while he was working at Google.

In 2014, Google and the Pokémon Company teamed up for an April Fools' Day joke that allowed viewers to find Pokémon creatures on Google maps. It was a viral hit, and Hanke started thinking the idea could be turned into a real game.

From December 2015 through February 2016, Hanke raised $25 million from Google, Nintendo, the Pokémon Company, and other investors to put together the team of more than forty people he would need to launch Pokémon Go.

In July 2016, Hanke and his team launched Pokémon Go. The app immediately became an overnight phe-nomenon, generating more than $2 million daily in in-app purchases.

How did John Hanke achieve his "overnight success?" By focusing, at each step, on the longer-term perspective. Each small step along the way led him to something just a little bit greater—until finally, he reached the phenomenal success of Pokémon Go.

CHOOSE TO BE OPTIMISTIC

Successful people believe they can do amazing things.

Optimism is not an exercise in fantasy,

but a reality-based belief system that leads us

to be active and effective in our lives,

working toward good outcomes while avoiding bad ones.

—CHRISTOPHER PETERSON & LISA BOSSIO

Recently, I ran into a woman who worked for me more than a decade ago. I was happy to see her, and I greeted her with whole-hearted warmth and friendliness. To my surprise, her response was chilly and stiff.

"What's up with her?" I later asked one of my employees.

"You really don't remember?"

I shook my head. In my mind, I had nothing but warm feelings for this woman.

"Well, you and she didn't exactly part company under the best of terms. She refused to do her job, and you had to fire her."

I don't have amnesia, and I'm not getting senile. When reminded, I did remember those events. But I had spent the last years working so hard at concentrating on the positive that my negative experience with my former employee had dropped out of my mind. Refusing to dwell on past painful situations—to the point of forgetting about them—has become so habitual for me that I call this behavior "delusional optimism."

I don't mean to be overly simplistic, but bad memories are like weeds in a garden. If you give them space, bad memories have a tendency not only to linger but also to expand in your mind, demanding your attention and tainting even your good thoughts. After obsessing way too many times on miserable memories, I learned that dwelling on the past doesn't get me any closer to my goals. So now I simply refuse to let the past intrude on my efforts to create a joyful present and successful future.

This doesn't mean that I don't acknowledge and deal with those difficult things as they arise. It just means that I face them, learn from them, and move on.

Choosing to focus on the best in yourself and in others is powerful behavior that creates positive results. Studies show that almost all successful people are optimists. I don't mean that successful people just have a naturally sunny outlook on life. No, I mean that they believe that good things *can* happen, and they choose to focus on that instead of all the negative things that have happened to them (and might happen again). This is not an unhealthy delusion. Instead, it's a healthy positive outlook that actually shapes the reality successful people experience.

Optimism is good for the body and soul, both literally and figuratively. Optimism and creating your Best Day Ever go hand-in-hand.

Martin Seligman, a psychologist who has studied optimists, reports that all optimists look at problems the same way. First, they believe that problems don't last forever. When negative things happen, they perceive them as temporary problems, not the kiss of doom that indicates that their entire life is destined for failure. Second, optimists believe that the problems they've experienced are pretty small in the grand scheme of things. They know that bad things can happen—employees may have to be fired, mistakes can be made, and the world economy can wobble—but nevertheless, they believe that overall life is good. No temporary failure, mistake, or conflict can ruin the entire big picture of life that they carry in their minds. Negative events seem minor (or even forgettable!) by comparison to their overall hope for the future.

Optimists shape their reality—as do pessimists. When we perceive reality a certain way, we act accordingly, and our actions often lead to the very thing we're expecting, either success or defeat. Alan Loy McGinnis, the author of *The Power of Optimism*, studied the biographies of more than a thousand successful people and found they were all optimists who had these things in common:

- They looked for partial solutions. They didn't think success is all or nothing. They were open to taking small steps that could lead to success.

- They used their imaginations to picture success. They played imaginary movies in their heads of what success will look like. (Successful athletes use this same technique.)

- They believed that no matter what their skills were now, they could improve them. They believed their personal best was yet to come, and they had confidence in their ability to grow.

Being optimistic won't change life's realities. If you're barely five feet tall, odds are fairly good you won't become a professional basketball player. If you're tone deaf, you're unlikely to become a famous musician. But optimism can allow you to use every bit of who you are to achieve the most possible.

The famous phrase "Keep Calm and Carry On" has been reproduced on posters, mugs, hats, shirts, and more over the past few years. But did you know that the saying is actually part of a three-part poster series that Britain used to buoy public spirits during the dark days of World War II? The poster series ended with the exhortation: "Your Courage, Your Cheerfulness, Your Resolution Will Bring Us Victory." The British government recognized the key role that attitude would play in winning the war—and the determination and cheerfulness of Britain's population through years of danger and destruction did in fact contribute to their ability to keep going against their enemies. Optimism is a choice that takes consistent, diligent practice. But if believing all things are possible is a key to unlocking an amazing future, then isn't it worth it?

BUSINESS APPLICATION

A psychologist at the University of Pennsylvania conducted studies that indicated that optimists are more successful than pessimists in the business world. Based on his research, Metropolitan Life, the insurance and financial services corporation, developed a test that allowed them to identify optimists and pessimists when they were hiring salespeople. After a year, when Metropolitan looked at both groups' records, the optimists outsold the pessimists by 20 percent. Then, during the second year, the difference jumped to 50 percent.

MAKE IT PERSONAL

- Do you consider yourself an optimist or a pessimist? Why?

- Examine yourself honestly. Where specifically have you let pessimism creep into your life?

- Pessimism writes a very different storyline from optimism. Rewrite the pessimistic storyline you just identified. Replace it with an optimistic storyline.

- In the days ahead, whenever you find yourself telling yourself a pessimistic story, consciously choose to replace it with an optimistic storyline.

Try writing these optimistic stories on index cards or on your phone's notes; refer to them often as you begin building your own version of habitual optimism.

 INSPIRATION

In 1912, author Christian D. Larson wrote this "Optimist's Creed":

Promise yourself . . .

To be so strong that nothing can disturb your peace of mind.

To talk health, happiness and prosperity to every person you meet.

To make all your friends feel that there is something in them.

To look at the sunny side of everything and make your optimism come true.

To think only of the best, to work only for the best and to expect only the best . . . .

To forget the mistakes of the past and press on to the greater achievements of the future.

To wear a cheerful countenance at all times and give every living creature you meet a smile.

To give so much time to the improvement of yourself that you have no time to criticize others.

To be too large for worry, too noble for anger, too strong for fear, and too happy to permit the presence of trouble.

To think well of yourself and to proclaim this fact to the world, not in loud words but great deeds.

To live in faith that the whole world is on your side so long as you are true to the best that is in you.

Believe in yourself and all that you are. Know that there is something inside you that is greater than any obstacle.

LOOK AT FAILURE FROM A NEW PERSPECTIVE

Use mistakes creatively.

You build on failure. You use it as a stepping stone . . . .
You don't try to forget the mistakes, but you don't dwell on it.
You don't let it have any of your energy,
or any of your time, or any of your space.

—**JOHNNY CASH**

A few years ago, the small company that handled our website came to me and said, "We're having a lot of internal struggles right now, and we are probably going to go out of business." This was not good news for me and my company, since 100 percent of our revenue is generated from our website.

"Of course we'll do our best to find a soft landing for you," the other company told me, "and find you someone else to work your website."

That wasn't a great solution. In the slow season, our website does between five hundred and seven hundred transactions a day—and over a thousand a day during the winter months. Finding a new relationship with a new website development company on short notice seemed daunting and scary.

"We can't have our website go down," I was thinking, "and we don't want to make a new relationship with someone under duress."

So, hoping for continuity, I asked the website company, "Can we just buy all your assets? We'd like to hire the people who are working on our website and assume ownership of their other accounts too."

And that's what we did. The deal had to be done quickly, so that there would be no interruption in our online service. The whole complicated agreement was put together in about forty-five days—from that first phone call to the day we signed the papers.

That turned out to be a mistake. The same structural problems that had been making the company's business flounder were all still there. Everywhere I turned, there were interpersonal and cultural problems—and I couldn't fix them. Years of infighting had led to a toxic workplace.

I had never walked into a company before and not felt excited to be at work, knowing that my team was behind me 100 percent. Now, not only did these new hires not support my efforts to help them, but they actively disliked me. They weren't thankful that I'd come to rescue them, and it didn't even seem like they liked their jobs much, with or without me. I had thought that if I just gave them raises, better equipment, and a nicer place to work, things would turn around.

But that didn't happen. I would have needed to build a new company from the ground up, so that my cultural norms and values would have been integrated into the structure. As it was, there was no way I could come into an established company that had been around for fifteen years and change things around quickly. Not only did it not work as I'd hoped, but it was making me miserable in the process. Adding insult to injury, the company was also losing money.

My goal had been to stabilize my company's website. Instead, I now owned a website company with twelve employees, plus other clients who were now also my responsibility. What was I going to do with it? I realized that I had to get myself out or it would hold back the rest of my business. But it wasn't easy.

It took me six months to stabilize our own website by moving it over to a large, capable company—and then it took another twelve months to get myself free from the website company I'd purchased. I had to get its clients transitioned to a new company; I had to either help the employees who were working there to find new jobs or help them negotiate new contracts with the company that ended up taking over everything. And during that time, the year during which I was shutting that company down and transitioning everything, it was bleeding cash.

In the end, I sold the website company at a loss. Meanwhile, the former owner from the original company had used much of the intellectual property that was developed with my money and went on to start a new company with that same intellectual property. I had to watch him use my investment to achieve success in his new venture. It was infuriating, frustrating, humiliating, and devastating.

This huge failure cost me financially, but it also cost me in other ways that were just as bad. Dealing with my mistake took my eye off the ball at Bramble Berry, my main company, which meant that my real business suffered. On top of that, the situation was personally stressful. Having my Best Day Ever became challenging. The only way I got through it was by working my way through five steps:

- I talked through my feelings with people whom I respect and admire. I didn't try to whitewash what had happened or soft sell how bad the failure had been—and they helped me see what I could learn from the experience.

- I accepted that there are some things in life I'm not good at—like running a software company—and then I focused on what I *am* good at. I'm really good at making soap; I'm really good at teaching and coaching; and I'm really good at working with women. So I doubled down on Bramble Berry and developed the Best-Day-Ever philosophy. Both allow me to use my true skills.

- I practiced all my Best-Day-Ever strategies even if I did not feel like it. I focused on finding joy in every single day, writing a gratitude journal, and assuming goodwill.

- I thought about skills I could develop to rebuild my self-confidence, and I worked to use my skills creatively, in outside-of-the-box ways. I'm firmly convinced that creativity combined with intentional happiness is a powerhouse for prosperity—and since learning new things is one of my skills that always lights me up, I went back to school to get my nutritional therapy certificate.

- I moved on. I stopped looking back over my shoulder, dwelling on the failure, and I looked expectantly toward the future. I made plans. I didn't let myself get stuck in regret and embarrassment; instead, I got excited about the goals that lay ahead.

There are a couple of recent business mantras that say, "Fail fast and fail often," and, "If you're not failing enough, you're not trying." I'm not sure I'd go that far. You don't want to use those mantras as an excuse for sloppiness or carelessness—for not doing your homework ahead of time. Sure, I learned a lot from my experience with that website company, but I also could have saved myself a lot of money and heartache if I'd taken time to find out more about the company before I bought it. A little research could have shown me how intractable and ingrained the problems were. I might also have consulted with experienced businesspeople I trust, who might have advised me to try another solution to the problem.

So here's what I'd say instead: "Failure is an opportunity to learn and grow—but you need to take all the steps possible to *not* fail." My experience taught me that, while we shouldn't let the fear of failure keep us from trying new things, we also need to keep Strategy #5 in mind—"Feet First, Not Head First." We can try to make our failures as cheap as possible by starting out small, rather than leaping into something that costs us more than we can comfortably afford if it turns out our investment doesn't pay off.

For example, it's one thing to say to yourself, "Hey, I want to learn how to ride a horse," so you sign up for horseback riding lessons, and you're out $250 for a month of lessons, and maybe another $250 for various clothes and equipment you buy for your new hobby. If it turns out you hate horseback riding—or that it's something you just can't master—$500 and four lessons could be an appropriate failure cost for your lifestyle. On the other hand, if instead you buy a horse, build a stable, and turn your yard into a fenced-in pasture—

and then decide that you don't really enjoy horseback riding—then you've probably invested a lot more than is comfortable!

Leaps of faith are often touted in our culture—but when you take a crazy leap out into thin air, there's no guarantee you won't end up smashed into pieces at the bottom of the cliff. How much you can afford to lose will depend on your personal circumstances; only you can determine the amount of money and time you are willing to sacrifice should your new venture flop. Figure out what that amount is *before* you take the leap, however, not after.

Make sure you have a safety net. Do you have another income source that will allow you to pay your living expenses if your new business doesn't make a profit for the next six years? If you decide to quit your job and go back to school, do you have a spouse with a job that will cover the income loss, who is also willing to pick up some of the household chores you'll no longer have time to manage? What's your backup plan in case your crazy, wonderful idea doesn't work out?

And here's another thing my failure experience taught me: There are always more options to choose from than are obvious at first. When the company managing Bramble Berry's website told me it was going out of business, I thought I had only two options: buy the company—or have our website go down and cost us millions of dollars in lost sales. But I've learned that there is always a third option (and maybe even a fourth and a fifth). It just takes some time and thought to find alternatives.

Finally, maybe the most important thing that failure taught me is that I didn't have to identify myself with it. Sure, I had to accept responsibility for my own decisions and actions—but they didn't have to define me.

Mistakes don't decrease your worth as a human being. They don't subtract from all the other things at which you excel. Learn as much as you can from these experiences. And then use them to make you stronger.

 BUSINESS APPLICATION

Two University of California-Berkeley business school professors, John Danner and Mark Coopersmith, have published a book called *The Other "F" Word* in which they offer seven steps for using failure as a valuable resource for business success.

1. Respect and anticipate failure in order to reduce the fear of it.

Acknowledge and accept that a certain amount of failure is inevitable. Coopersmith told *Business Insider*, "In order to turn [failure] from a recurring regret into a strategic resource, companies have to stop denying and ignoring it."

2. Rehearse to improve your reflexes.

Coopersmith and Danner suggest applying what they call the "Un-Golden Rule" to your business: "Do unto yourself before others can do unto you." Imagine ahead of time what failure could look like— and think through solutions. "Companies should regularly and creatively assess their own most fragile vulnerabilities before those are exposed and exploited by competitors eager to capture customers and market share," Danner says.

3. Recognize failure's signals earlier to buy time.

Instead of ignoring early warning signs, you can use these to help buy your company time to make better decisions that will minimize the effects of failure. Coopersmith and Danner recommend rewarding customers, suppliers, and employees for identifying situations worth fixing or improving.

4. React quickly to minimize damage.

Have a plan already in place for how your company will cope with failure. Despite the need for quick reaction, however, Coopersmith and Danner also recommend making time "to clearly understand the situation and assemble your response."

5. Reflect to draw insights.

Treat failure like feedback that can be a positive resource. Danner says that we should ask, "What, why, how, where, and when?"—rather than, "Who was responsible?" This will engage employees in useful conversation (rather than assigning blame), and you'll be able to develop "a response which has positive implications for culture, productivity, and the ability to better incorporate those insights and people in the next stage."

6. Rebound to put new action plans into play to improve performance.

Lead your "troops" back onto the field with increased wisdom, seeing this as an opportunity to perform even better.

7. Remember to strengthen workplace culture.

Use failure to build stories and other reminders you can incorporate into your business' routines, reports, and physical environment.

In a video about their book, the authors talk about Instagram as an example of a company that has successfully gone through the steps they list in their book. When the Instagram founders talked to their early customers, they discovered that their site was too complicated. The customers did, however, say that they loved the photo section of the app—so the founders went back and created the photo app that grew to 150 million users. If they had given up when their customers told them, "This product is a failure. It's too complicated, and we're not sure how to use it," then they would have closed up shop. Instead, they listened and asked not only, "What's failing?" but also, "What can we identify that's a success? What can we learn from this?"

Danner and Coopersmith also point to WD-40 as a company that repeatedly failed—thirty-nine times to be exact—but has since grown into a $1.3 billion business.

What can failure teach you about your business?

 MAKE IT PERSONAL

- Describe a failure you experienced that still stings whenever you think of it.

- Now take some time to think about the positive lessons you can pull from this experience. What did you learn? How has it made you stronger? How can you build something better out of this failure?

 INSPIRATION

When Harland Sanders was forty years old, he opened a service station where he also cooked chicken and other Southern dishes. The service station had no seating, so people ate in his adjacent living quarters. His cooking became so popular that he eventually moved into a nearby motel and opened a 142-seat restaurant.

He was pan-frying his chicken, but this meant that each order took him thirty minutes to prepare, so he started working to perfect the use of a pressure fryer to cook his chicken faster. After plenty of failures along the way, finally, nine years later, he released his new chicken—which he discovered had a flakier crust and juicier meat than pan-fried—with a new blend of spices (known today as "Original Recipe").

Harland—now known as "Colonel Sanders"—had a booming business for the next sixteen years. Then his restaurant took a massive hit when an interstate highway was built that rerouted traffic away from it. Eventually, Harland had to accept that his business was now a failure. He sold the restaurant at auction and got just enough to cover his debts. At age sixty-five, after twenty-five successful years in the restaurant business, Colonel Sanders was broke.

But he hadn't given up. After he received his first Social Security check for $105, he hit the road looking for restaurants to buy the rights to his recipe. For the next two years, he lived in his car—and every single day, when he offered his recipe for sale, someone told him no. He was rejected 1,009 times before he finally found a restaurant owner who agreed to use his recipe.

Colonel Sanders licensed his recipe and received 5 cents per chicken in return. After seven years, when he was seventy-four years old, his chicken was being sold in six hundred restaurants in the US and Canada. Then, at age seventy-five, Colonel Sanders became a millionaire when he sold Kentucky Fried Chicken for $2 million. He had never thought of failure as permanent—and now, despite friends and family who never believed he could do it, all his failures had led to success.

Franklin D. Roosevelt once said, "It is not the critic who counts; not the man who points out how the strong man stumbles or where the doer of deeds could have done them better. The credit belongs to the man who is actually in the arena, whose face is marred by dust and sweat and blood; who strives valiantly; who errs, who comes short again and again, because there is no effort without error and shortcoming; but who does actually strive to do the deeds; who knows great enthusiasms, the great devotions; who spends himself in a worthy cause; who at the best knows in the end the triumph of high achievement, and who at the worst, if he fails, at least fails while daring greatly, so that his place shall never be with those cold and timid souls who neither know victory nor defeat."

Colonel Sanders dared greatly—and in the end, he knew the triumph of high achievement.

#9

GIVE IT ALL YOU'VE GOT—AND THEN SOME

Break free of the self-limitations you've imposed on yourself.

When you look in the mirror, what do you see?

Do you see the real you,

or what you have been conditioned to believe is you?

The two are so, so different.

One is an infinite consciousness

capable of being and creating whatever it chooses,

the other is an illusion imprisoned

by its own perceived and programmed limitations.

—DAVID ICKE

I recently had a mentoring session with a smart woman I'll call Jan. She had been out of work for a while but had finally landed a job. The salary was 50 percent less than what she wanted to be paid, but at least it was a job. Only a few weeks into her new work, however, she realized her new company had problems; in fact, it was a serious mess.

Jan knew she had the skills to help the company dramatically, but she also knew she was not being paid what her help was worth. She didn't want to be taken advantage of. She worried that her boss would take her efforts and never reward them financially.

So Jan asked my advice: Should she make a difference in her new role, even though she wasn't being paid for it—or only do what she was being paid to do? She'd been burned before by unscrupulous employers, and she didn't want to make herself vulnerable in that way again.

At first, I was utterly baffled by the idea that Jan would intentionally hold herself back. But as Jan and I talked about her situation more, we realized something: Her dilemma was about her, not her boss and whatever he might or might not do. She could play it safe and hide her true worth—but she would be limiting herself far more than she would be protecting herself.

Ultimately, my advice was to try to expand her role and show her value to her employer. If that value wasn't being recognized, she could look for another job, but in the meantime, she would be growing and learning—and who knows what unexpected opportunities her experience might lead to down the road?

Sometimes we kid ourselves that we're practicing sensible caution, getting into the pool feet first instead of head first (Strategy #5), when really we're just afraid of giving life all we've got. We can be totally committed while still taking small, careful steps. Growth requires courage. It's an adventure; it's an ongoing process of innovation and creativity.

The world doesn't need people who are hiding under a bushel. It wants people to shine and go forth with their special abilities, talents, and energy. All of us (including me) have experiences that hold us back. Because we were hurt in the past, we try to protect ourselves against those same wounds reoccurring in our current lives. In my case, before I developed my habit of "delusional optimism," I struggled to move past the experience of feeling rejected by my middle school's cliques. How silly is it that certain things kids said to me so many years ago could have the power to hold me back! (Of course, they didn't deserve that power, and now I won't allow them to have it.)

All of us have wounds like that, injuries to our self-concepts that we've absorbed so deeply we act as though they're today's reality.

It's not Suzy Jones from middle school who threatens to derail my success, and neither is it Jan's employers, either past or present, who are holding her back. Ultimately, it's *me* who sets limits on what I can do, just as Jan was setting limits on her own achievements.

Stop listening to those old voices in your head. You can choose to live a new reality. Whatever flaws you have won't magically go away—but you can learn to work with them. You can grow in amazing ways, reaching out to your full potential.

Isn't it time to give the world all you've got?

 BUSINESS APPLICATION

In 1519, the Spanish Conquistador Hernando Cortés and his eleven ships landed on the shores of the Yucatan Peninsula in what is now Mexico. They were far from home, and many of them must have been scared of the unknown world they encountered—so their hearts must have really sunk when Cortés announced that he was burning the ships. Retreat was no longer possible. They had to commit totally to Cortés' vision.

We all cling to something that makes us feel safe. We postpone action until we no longer feel fear, or we make shallow attempts never designed to succeed. To truly achieve the level of success we each desire, there are times when we need to "burn the ships."

Business coach Travis Roberts recommends looking at the following "ships" to determine if one of them needs burning:

Your current job: Are you so comfortable where you are that you're afraid to step out of your rut and try something new, something that might be more creative and fulfilling, something that would align your life more closely with the things you value most? Do note, however, that "burning your ship" does NOT mean quitting your job without a safety net. Instead, it can include strategies from #5 (Feet First, Not Head First and A Deeper Dive: Embrace the Power of the Trudge).

Your field of employment: Have you been dreaming of a career change? Do you tell yourself, "It wouldn't make sense to do that?" Maybe you invested years and money getting the education this field requires. Maybe it just seems too scary to walk away from financial security and try something else. But does this field make you feel disconnected from the values you hold most dear?

A bad business deal: Sometimes we stick with a bad business relationship, determined to make it work, because we don't want to admit that we made a mistake. If there's a relationship like that in your professional life, ask yourself: Why can't you let it go? Would it be better for everyone concerned if you burned this ship?

An unrealistic dream: Sometimes we can't let go of a dream, even though life keeps telling us it will never come true. It's one thing to keep working against the odds in order to achieve something great—but it's another thing altogether to keep trying something for which we truly lack the abilities or resources. Make sure your goals aren't just fantasies that are impossible to achieve. Be realistic enough to burn a dream that could be getting in your way of discovering a practical way to match your values with your goals.

Keep in mind, though, that the point of "burning these ships" isn't just to give up and die. Cortés burned his ships so he and his men would be freed from ties to the past, able to commit themselves without reserve to the future. We too need to examine our careers and businesses to identify anything that is holding us back. When we identify and free ourselves from those things, we will be able to give our all to becoming the best we can be in our professional lives.

MAKE IT PERSONAL

Ask yourself three important questions: Where do you hold yourself back? What patterns have you learned that have protected you in the past but are hurting you now? How are your beliefs about yourself and others limiting your true potential? If you ask yourself these questions and then commit to answering them by writing longhand for thirty straight minutes, no interruptions, you may be very surprised by your deeply honest response.

Reaching these answers is the first part of the battle. You will begin to feel your own potential more fully once you realize what self-limiters you've placed on yourself without even knowing it.

INSPIRATION

As you work at recognizing and breaking free from hidden self-limitations, a book you might find helpful is *Are You Ready to Succeed? Unconventional Strategies to Achieving Personal Mastery in Business and Life* by Srikumar S. Rao.

Rao describes "mental models" that dictate how you act and how you interpret the events in your life. "When you change the model," Rao says, "you change your life."

Rao explains that when we interpret our current lives, we are often influenced by "old data," rather than the actual data from the present situation. In other words, we are controlled by what our old boss did or said rather than our current boss—or, in my case, we are listening to a middle school kid instead of paying attention to today's reality.

Recognize your mental models, Rao advises, and then evaluate each one using this criterion: Does it help you achieve your ends? Don't worry about whether it's true or not, he says; that's not nearly as important as whether it helps you to move forward toward your goals. If it doesn't—then, says Rao, drop that mental model. You don't need it. It's just getting in your way.

#10

OVERUSED STRENGTHS CAN BECOME WEAKNESSES

The skill sets that got you here may not be what will get you to the next level.

Any virtue carried to an extreme can become a crime.

—ALEXANDER DUMAS

A few years ago, as I was describing a work situation to my business mentor, he suddenly put up his hand to stop me. Feeling pretty good about my ability to be organized, linear, and thoughtful, I'd been telling him, "These are the five things I'm going to do. This is what I'm doing next. This is how it's going to work out. This is what I'm doing after that . . . ." So I was truly astounded when he said to me, "Anne-Marie, you are like a robot. Life doesn't always work like that."

At first, I couldn't wrap my head around what he was saying. Ever since I was young, I've been rewarded for being so organized. I'd taken pride in the praise I got from my teachers and parents for being the girl who could juggle two part-time jobs, volunteer activities, and her schoolwork. In high school, I actually carried a Franklin Covey's day planner with me everywhere I went! As a teenager, I'd already learned the hard way that having a well-organized, planned-out life is the only way to manage big projects and goals. A commitment to an organized life is essential to living my Best Day Ever. Instead of taking away flexibility and freedom, organization actually gives me *more* freedom. If occasionally, I wish to skip something on my schedule in order to play an extra three hours with my kids, I can do so, because I know exactly what I need to do to make up for the time I lost: I'll have to look at my schedule and fit those three hours of time in somewhere else.

Organizational skills are a learned skill that helped get me to a good place as an adult today. But now, my mentor had just referred to me as a "robot," and his comments made it sound like my organizational skills were a flaw rather than a strength.

Yet that's not what he meant. He had an important lesson for me to learn, and it was this: Sometimes, when we overuse certain skills (especially those that come easily for us), our greatest strengths can turn into weaknesses or even crutches that hobble more than help us. For example, the more stressed I am, the more organized I get; it's how I handle a crisis, by making a to-do list, and then pushing through it. But my mentor saw what I was doing, and he realized that my obsession with a plan causes the people around me to be *more* stressed, and I was failing to see it. What I perceived as careful, linear thinking, he was seeing as rigid thinking; what I thought was necessary structure, he identified as a box that was frustrating—and sometimes locking out—those around me.

Once I'd opened my mind to the possibility that a strength could also be a weakness, I started recognizing something similar in other areas of my life. For example, people have always given me a lot of emotional reinforcement for being the Best-Day-Ever Girl, the enthusiastic, cheerful person who tries to see the best in every person and situation. I've been praised and rewarded so much for being Little Miss Sunshine that it's become the persona I automatically wear all the time. It's a genuine part of my personality, yes, but sometimes that cheerleader's uniform can turn into a forbidding armor without my realizing it.

Let's say I'm bouncing around doing my "Hey, it's the best day ever!" thing and then someone says to me, "Sorry, Anne-Marie, I'm just not in the mood for your cheeriness today. My dog just died. My husband is in the hospital. I'm really sad, and this is definitely not my best day ever."

Sometimes people don't need a cheerleader. Sometimes what they need most is empathy. They need someone who is willing to shed a tear with them, to simply be present with them in their sadness or anxiety. My preoccupation with Best-Day-Ever thinking can be a barrier, one that prevents authentic relationships from forming with people who need to trust me with the reality of their lives.

Being super-competitive is another trait of mine that has helped push me toward success. Yet it can be both a strength and a detriment. Becoming and remaining a successful businessperson has demanded that I examine my personal strengths—including my competitiveness—and pay attention to where those "strengths" are holding me back rather than moving me closer to my long-term goals.

As my business grew, I noticed, for example, that my employee turnover was higher than I wanted it to be. I knew I needed to be a better leader, and that meant taking a close look at myself in the mirror. When I did, I realized that the high standards I set for myself—my need to excel at everything I do—made me impatient with what I perceived as weakness in others. If I got to work early, I was disappointed if I was the only one there. If I had to redo work that a team member did, I would be impatient about it. When I provided feedback, I was rushed and short with people. Needless to say, employees don't enjoy working for a boss who is frequently impatient and stingy with compliments. In a negative work environment, team members will start looking for a job where they feel they'll be appreciated, where they won't dread coming to work every morning. Learning to be less competitive at work was a painful lesson I had to learn.

One more example: I'm a fast and enthusiastic speaker. I *love* to express myself verbally. This means I've never been afraid of public speaking. It means I'm comfortable presenting my ideas out loud to all kinds of people. And you know what else it means? It means I talk too darn much. I end up steamrolling people in meetings, not always giving them the chance to contribute their ideas and feedback to whatever we're discussing.

Your strengths may not be mine. In fact, they might be just the opposite of mine. For example, maybe you were reinforced as a young person for your caring and empathy, for your ability to listen to others' problems, and for your sensitivity to their emotions. Those are wonderful abilities to have. But now let's say you're running your own business, and your empathy for your employees means you're not able to ever hold them to any standard. You're so quick to see their point of view and feel their pain that you can't also balance the realistic demands of running a business. When an employee's dog dies, you feel so badly for him that you let him take off a week from work. You hear someone sniffle as you walk through the office, so you send her home and tell her to take a nap for the rest of the day. Or you have an employee who simply can't do the job, but you keep him on your payroll because you don't want to hurt his feelings. Being overly sensitive to others' feelings can hurt your business as much as being not sensitive enough can.

What it comes down to is this: We all have certain skills we learned when we were young, things that were our selling points in life, the qualities our parents and teachers and friends stroked us for in one way or another. Those skills helped get us to the place where we're at today. But now, it's time to go further.

Imagine you're leading a team that's building a house. You are really good at pounding nails. You *love* pounding nails. In fact, you can pound nails faster than almost anyone else. So you keep telling everyone, "Come on, people! Let's get these nails pounded! I'll show you how, and then you'll be able to pound nails like me." So there you all are, pounding nails like crazy. And that's great when you're at the stage where you're building the framework of the house. It's also a pretty useful skill when you're laying the flooring and putting up drywall. But now it's time to take your house to the next level. If you want to build a beautiful place for someone to live and thrive, then you better develop some other skills besides pounding nails—like paying attention to *interior* design, picking out calming or energizing paint colors, and being conscious of the circulation of light and fresh air.

I'm not saying I need to stop being organized or you should stop being empathetic. Those are both important strengths to have, ones that will continue to serve us well. But instead of responding automatically with our habitual skill sets, we need to become more sensitive to what each circumstance in life actually requires. We need to practice a more realistic awareness of each moment, as well as self-awareness, understanding when and how to use the skills we have—and when to set them aside and work at developing new strengths.

BUSINESS APPLICATION

In a 2009 issue of the *Harvard Business Review*, business researchers Robert E. Kaplan and Robert B. Kaiser reported their study of the effects of overused management strengths on two aspects of team performance: vitality (defined as morale, engagement, and cohesion) and productivity (quantity and quality of output). Here's what they found: "Taking a strength to an extreme is always detrimental to performance, but even a mild tendency to overdo it can be harmful. Be a little too forceful, for instance, and your team's output may improve some—but vitality will take a hit, and weakened morale will eventually undercut productivity. Be a little too enabling, and you may shore up vitality—but productivity will suffer over time, which will in turn erode morale. In general, overdoing it hurts your effectiveness just as much as *under*doing it."

 MAKE IT PERSONAL

- Look at the chart below and identify two or three of your strongest personal qualities. If you don't see them already on the chart, then add them at the bottom—and then think about how each can be both a strength and a potential weakness.

PERSONAL QUALITY	STRENGTH	POTENTIAL WEAKNESS
Excitable	Enthusiastic about new projects	Becomes upset by criticism or negative circumstances
Cautious	Careful, makes fewer mistakes	Unwilling to take necessary risks
Idealistic	High standards for achievement	Can become paralyzed by perfectionism
Reserved	Capable of working alone	Too aloof and detached from others
Self-confidence	Ambitious and willing to try hard tasks	Self-absorbed, arrogant, unwilling to acknowledge mistakes
Imaginative	Creative, outside-the-box thinker	Impractical, eccentric ("weird")
Sensitive	Eager to please	Too reliant on others' opinions
Cooperativeness	Good team player	Avoids necessary conflicts
Independent	Stands up for beliefs	Unable to compromise
Goal-oriented	Gets things done	Steamrolls over others
Verbal	Communicates well	Talks too much
Organized	Plans effectively	Loses spontaneity
Patience	Endures hardship, able to wait for results	Complacent with the status quo

- Now, describe the ways in which you have been rewarded for these qualities. How have they helped to get you where you are today?

- Spend a few moments being as honest as you can with yourself. Are one or more of these qualities holding you back at this stage in your life? How?

- What strength do you need to develop to meet the current circumstances of your life? List at least three things you can begin doing now to practice this new strength.

INSPIRATION

Dan Rockwell (who blogs about the qualities of a good leader) has this to say about preventing our greatest strengths from becoming our greatest weaknesses:

If you are a great talker, you talk too much.

Listen more.

If you are a great listener, you listen too much.

Talk more.

If you are great at execution, you rely too much on getting things done.

Dream more.

If you are a dreamer, you launch too quickly.

Execute more.

If you are great at encouraging, people walk all over you.

Confront more.

If you are great at discernment, you walk over others.

Comfort more.

If you are great at organization, you're inflexible.

Adapt more.

If you are creative, you're scatterbrained.

Ask more questions.

If you are a detail person, you're rigid.

Try new things more.

Your greatest strength makes you interesting and useful. Use it, follow it, and leverage it for the good of others. However, it doesn't take long for a one-string banjo to irritate any listener. You'll reach higher by adding a few strings to your instrument.

A DEEPER DIVE: WELCOMING FEEDBACK THAT REVEALS YOUR BLIND SPOTS

Honest criticism offers a chance to grow.

We all have blind spots—
those areas for improvement and growth.
As painful as it can be to admit
we're doing things we never wanted to do
and saying things we never wanted to say,
it is this acknowledgement that enables you
to take the first step toward change.
Be gentle with yourself. Be real with yourself.
Take baby steps.

—RHONDA LOUISE ROBBINS

Imagine you're getting ready to go to a formal event, rushing around so fast you don't even notice the dress you slipped over your head has a large jelly stain on the back of it. You look at yourself in the mirror and smile: The dress looks great on you. You head for the door, feeling confident that you're looking your best.

Before you get too far, however, a friend grabs you by the arm. "Honey," she says while pulling you aside, "you can't wear that dress!"

"How come?" you demand, more than a little irritated. You love the dress, and you know you look good in it.

"Because," your friend answers, "there's a big stain on it. See?"

She pushes you to a mirror, then holds up a hand mirror so you can see the stain on the back of the dress. Needless to say, you find something else to wear.

Thank goodness for good friends who care enough to tell us the truth! Just as it's impossible for us to see (without a little help) the back of our favorite dress once we're wearing it, it's also hard to recognize when a personality strength has tipped over into a weakness.

We all have blind spots of various sorts and sizes. These are not the list of flaws that we're aware we have. By definition, we can't see our blind spots, so we don't know what they are. Of course, certain practices encourage us to see ourselves more clearly (acting as mirrors to the parts of ourselves that are hidden from our view), but self-awareness is a slow process when we practice it alone. A way to speed up the process is to start paying close attention to how people respond to us when we're exercising what we consider to be our strengths. Their reactions can tell us a lot about how well those strengths are serving us in our journey toward making every day our Best Day Ever.

We can accelerate the process even more if we ask people around us to give us feedback. Seeking out honest feedback like this feels terribly risky; it can seem as though we're making ourselves vulnerable in ways we don't want to be. It's a little like a skydiving dream where you suddenly realize that not only are you about to jump out of a plane that's hundreds of feet up in the air, but you are also stark naked. Staying on the ground fully clothed seems like a far safer and more sensible thing to do.

But feedback doesn't have to be dangerous, and it doesn't have to be a threat to our self-confidence. Instead, we can think of it simply as data that allows us to see what's working in our lives and what isn't—so that we can then adjust our behaviors accordingly. Smart marketers use feedback from focus groups to ensure they're communicating their product's value in the most effective way. By welcoming constructive criticism, you're just conducting an ongoing, highly informal focus group on yourself!

Most people won't volunteer this sort of feedback if we don't ask for it. We've all been trained to say nice things to people, and we know that negative feedback can create conflicts and hurt feelings. If we want people to help us to identify our blind spots, then we're going to have to specifically ask them to do so—and then not punish them in any way if they say something we don't like hearing.

It takes humility (and a bit of a thick skin) to do this. I remember the first time I asked my team to tell me two things they really like about me—and then two things they really *don't* like. Some of their answers were painful, I admit, but I learned important things about myself. (So much so that I've done it again a few times, although the answers never get easier to hear.)

Sometimes our coworkers can be more objective about us than the people who love us best. However, our partners and closest friends, if pressed to go beyond the obvious "you never throw out the trash" level of complaint, are often the people who can really help us most when it comes to identifying our true blind spots. After all, they know us best and still love us, warts and all.

I depend on my husband for this sort of feedback. I know now that my lack of empathy is a weakness, but that doesn't mean I can always recognize when a situation calls for greater sensitivity on my part. When my kids fall down and cry, I may sound less sympathetic than they need their mother to be. My natural inclination is to avoid coddling them, because focusing too much on the tears only magnifies the negative and detracts from building healthy resilience. So my response is often, "Get up! You're fine!"—until my husband points out to me that the situation calls for empathy rather than impatience and a would-be lesson in resilience. With my husband's feedback, I work as hard as I can at putting myself inside their heads when they need to me to understand their feelings. I don't want my blind spots to keep me from showing them all the love and support they need from me.

Will we ever be able to see *all* our blind spots? No, we won't. It will always be a work in progress, but that shouldn't stop us from striving to find as many as we can.

 MAKE IT PERSONAL

- Pick three people you trust and explain to them that you are honestly seeking their help in discovering your blind spots. If possible, choose people from different areas of your life, who see you in different settings (for example, a family member, a close friend, and a professional colleague). If you're nervous, do this over a hike or a coffee. Ask each of them these two questions and later write down their answers:

  □ "Do you see me using one of my strengths in a way that isn't helpful to others?"

  □ "Do you see something I don't recognize about myself that is holding me back?"

- How do you feel about this feedback? (It's okay to feel hurt, irritation, or frustration at first. Most of us do! Just don't let yourself get stuck in those emotions.)

- Now turn your focus to how you're going to use this feedback to improve your life. Describe steps you can take immediately to begin doing things differently. Refer back to this exercise often in the days and weeks to come. You don't want those blind spots to slip out of sight again.

PART II

Take Control of Your Life!

Plan for success.

#11

FIND YOUR "WHY"

When you're clear on what's important to you, it will give direction to your life.

*Your purpose in life is to find your purpose
and give your whole heart and soul to it.*

—GAUTAMA BUDDHA

I'm a firm believer that books can change lives. During those dreary days after my divorce, when I was battling illness and sadness, I spent a lot of time reading Stephen Covey's *The 7 Habits of Highly Effective People*. I give that book credit for helping me to tell myself a story of success and possibility rather than failure.

Covey's second habit is this: "Begin with the end in mind." What he means by this is that we need to understand *why* we are doing something. For example, if we are constructing a house, we need to know what a well-built house is like. If we are dieting, we need to understand what a healthy, fit body is like and figure out the hook—the "why" for wanting that. If we are in business, we need to be clear as to what we hope our business will achieve in the world. We make better choices and live more effectively when we know what the larger purpose is behind our actions. In his book, Covey takes this a step further and teaches his readers how to turn their "why" into a mission statement.

I knew I wasn't going to get through those difficult weeks and months after my marriage ended without a clear focus—but to *be* focused I needed to *find* my focus. All the hard work in the world wasn't going to get me anywhere if I didn't have a clear destination in mind. I needed a personal North Star, a guiding light I could aim for even when everything else was completely dark. I needed to know my "why."

In his book, Covey stressed that the first step toward understanding your "why" in life is to understand what your values are. We talk about values sometimes as though they're synonymous with moral concepts (integrity, compassion, loyalty, and so on). But our values are simply the things that are most important to us. My core values were the things that motivated me to get up in the morning. They're the things I hoped people would remember about me when I was no longer in their lives.

"When you discover your mission," wrote W. Clement Stone, "you will feel its demand. It will fill you with enthusiasm and a burning desire to get to work on it." I wanted that enthusiasm, and I needed the fuel of a burning desire—so at twenty-seven years old, I sat down to write my personal mission statement, the sentence that would summarize the entire plotline of my life. With my life falling apart, it was clear I needed something to guide me through the chaos of my life. I needed a destination to aim toward, a consistent point where I could fix my attention beyond whatever was going on in the moment.

Here's what I finally wrote as my mission statement: "My purpose is to use my enthusiasm for life and forward-thinking positivity to motivate, teach and inspire others to experience joy and fulfillment in their everyday lives."

That's still my calling. To this day, it's what guides everything thing that I do. It's my "why," the reason I get up every day, encapsulated in words I can look at whenever I'm confused or discouraged. I reread it when I'm having a bad day—or a bad week or a bad month—and it reminds me why I do what I do.

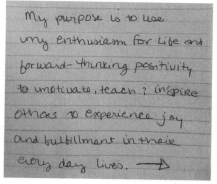

My original mission statement written on a note pad.

Having it first and foremost in my mind helps me focus on the things that matter most during my day; it keeps me from getting bogged down in minutia, because I always have this litmus test: "Will this behavior, will this action, help me inspire others? Or will it not? Is this action moving me closer to my mission?"

Of course, everyone's life has practical details that have to be attended to—like paying bills and doing laundry—but when you know what your overall mission is, it's easier to stay focused on the big picture. You don't have to spend so much time getting sidetracked by unimportant things.

And you have more room in your life for happiness.

BUSINESS APPLICATION

Simon Sinek's book *Start with Why* builds on Stephen Covey's ideas, but Sinek focuses specifically on success in business: "People don't buy what you do," he wrote, "they buy why you do it. And what you do simply proves what you believe." He goes on to say, "All organizations start with WHY, but only the great ones keep their WHY clear year after year."

If you're an entrepreneur, the "why" is the well-spring from which all of your actions, products, hiring decisions, and business interactions spring. Why does your organization exist? In your career, a strong "why" statement helps you decide where to work, whom to work for, and when to change careers, companies, or roles. Why do you get out of bed in the morning?

As Simon Sinek stated in his famous 2009 TED Talk, "This is about thinking, acting, and communicating from the inside out."

 MAKE IT PERSONAL

- To identify your values, first write the names of six people you admire. It doesn't matter if you know them personally. They could be people you've only read about or people from history.

- Now write down five adjectives (words that describe personal characteristics) for each of those people. You should end up with thirty adjectives.

- Next, pick your top five personal characteristics from the adjectives list, things that represent the qualities and standards you believe are most important. These might also be the five words you would hope would be used in your obituary to describe you. Rank them from 1 to 5 (1 being the most important, 5 being the least). These words represent your core values. Look at them for a while and think about what each word means to you. Come back to this list often in the future. Your core values don't usually change much over the years, so this list can be a constant that guides you toward the right path—and gives you a prod when you're slipping off from it. (This exercise is adapted from Stephen Covey's *The 7 Habits of Highly Effective People.* I encourage you to read his book for yourself.)

- Before you write your own personal mission statement, take time to think through what's most important to you and what it is you want most to achieve in life. Think about these questions:

  - What do you want from life?
  - What are you good at?
  - What gives you the most joy?
  - How do you want to be remembered?

- Combine the answers to those questions with your values—and now write the sentence or sentences that will be your own personal mission statement. It doesn't need to be perfect your first time. You can refine and change this over time.

 INSPIRATION

Henry David Thoreau is famous for escaping to the woods on Walden Pond in order to live a life that was closer to nature. His reason for doing this, though, was that he was seeking to understand what his values truly were, and he believed that so long as he was surrounded by "ordinary life," it would be hard for him to hear the voice of what was calling to him. He did not want to die, he wrote, only to discover that he had not really lived—and so, in the woods, he determined to avoid "all that was not life."

For Thoreau, "not life" was made up of all the unimportant things that clutter our lives. Most of us are not going to become hermits living alone in the woods in order to discover and practice our values— but Thoreau's experience does underline the fact that you have to carve a space in your life that's big enough for your values to take shape. That might mean setting aside an hour or two every Sunday to think about what is most important to you. It might mean taking fifteen minutes every morning. But without those small, intentional moments, your values' voices will be drowned out by the same "wearisome" noise that so bothered Thoreau.

At the end of Thoreau's time on Walden Pond, he was able to write: "I learned this, at least, by my experiment: that if one advances confidently in the direction of his dreams, and endeavors to live the life which he has imagined, he will meet with a success unexpected in common hours."

We too may find the same success when we let our values guide our lives.

A DEEPER DIVE:
A GOOD MISSION STATEMENT
FOCUSES YOUR PLANS

Align the details of your life with the big picture you've chosen.

You've got to think about big things while you're doing small things, so that all the small things go in the right direction.

—ALVIN TOFFLER

Imagine you wanted to travel to the North Pole. You could go outside at night and start walking, using the North Star as your guide. But you probably wouldn't get very far. You could walk and walk, and years later, you'd still be out there, staring at that distant star in the sky.

But if you *really* wanted to go to the North Pole, then you'd need to make plans. You'd figure out each step of the journey. You'd find the airport closest to the Arctic Circle and buy a plane ticket there. You'd also figure out how you would travel from the airport. Maybe you'd make arrangements for a dogsled to take you the rest of the way. Or maybe a snowmobile tour could take you north. You'd figure out expenses, and where you would sleep, and what you would eat. A trip that big would require lots of planning.

Your personal mission statement is pretty much the same. Once you've found your personal North Star, then the next step is to set milestones for yourself so you know you're making progress. No matter how much you think about your mission, things don't happen simply because you think about them. They happen because you *do* them. And that takes planning. It requires intentionally lining up the day-to-day actions in your life so that they always lead you closer to your mission, the reason you were put on this earth.

Each year, I sit down and outline my goals for the months ahead. During these planning sessions, my team and I create a set of goals for the business, my husband and I make goals for our family, and then I make another set for myself—but they all interlock, because all the spheres of my life work together to create the life I want to lead. Each of these goals will help me move closer to my overall personal mission, some of them more directly than others.

At first glance, you might think that some of my annual goals don't have all that close of a connection to my mission statement ("To use my enthusiasm for life and forward-thinking positivity to motivate, teach, and inspire others to experience joy and fulfillment in their everyday lives"). But what I'm really doing is intentionally building routines that will be like flights of stairs to help me reach my ultimate mission.

For example, for me to be able to use my forward-thinking positivity to inspire people, I have to bounce out of bed with energy. I genuinely must have enough in my personal fuel tank to be able to share it with others. I have to have enough love, joy, happiness, abundance, and good cheer so that I can write a blog post, go speak to a group of women, give a keynote address to six hundred women, or do a YouTube show on how to make soap. I must be energetic—and I can't be energetic without attending to my physical and emotional needs. I've discovered I need annual goals to help me do that in the most effective ways.

In 2016, one of my goals was to learn how to do the splits. You might say, "What does that possibly have to do with your mission statement?" But the goal wasn't really about the splits; it was about everything I would have to do in order to be able to do splits. I would have to stretch every single day. I would have to get into a yoga habit every week. I was going to need to take care of the little things that make my body flexible, not just the exercise that I naturally gravitate toward, like running on a treadmill because that's fun and easy, and I get quick results. Taking care of my body like that means I'm in my best physical shape—and that allows me to have the strength and energy I need for the grueling marathon of getting on a plane in the morning to give a keynote address that afternoon, then flying home again that night, and being happy, loving Super Mom the next morning.

Sometimes, though, I think we don't get much closer to our big life mission because we forget that we're the essential component. We see this big, lofty goal, and we focus on all the things we must do to get there, without realizing that we'll never reach any of our milestones if we don't have the strength we need for the journey. It would be like mapping the route we were going to run for a marathon, without bothering to get ourselves in shape before the run.

Joyful, energetic lives don't happen by accident. They take planning, work, and follow-through. My work and my family inspire me to create the best life possible for them and myself. They're worth it.

Your work and family deserve that same level of intention and commitment. And so do you!

 MAKE IT PERSONAL

I like to set my goals and plan my year at New Year's—but if you're reading this book in March—or

October or whenever—don't wait until then to set goals for yourself. Start now.

With your personal mission statement and values and North Star "Why" in front of you, think about where you would like to be in five years. Outline the major points here. These are your five-year goals.

Now think about what you can do in the next year to get yourself closer to your five-year goals. List those things here. These are your one-year goals.

Next, break down your one-year goals into three-month segments. List here what you can accomplish in the first, second, third, and fourth quarters of the year ahead.

Finally, break down your quarterly goals month by month and week by week. This is your twelve-month plan.

Copy your goals and plans into a twelve-month planner (either online or use the old-fashioned paper kind) where you can refer to them daily.

#12

MAKE YOUR PERSONAL MISSION STATEMENT UNFORGETTABLE

Use practical tools to integrate your personal mission into every single day.

Vision is the art of seeing the invisible.

—JONATHAN SWIFT

The North Star wouldn't be any use to navigators if they never looked at it—and neither is a personal mission statement if it sits forgotten in a book on your shelf. We need to make sure our mission statements are always somewhere visible, somewhere we can easily see them so we can use them to set our course.

My mission statement has stayed the same ever since I made it—but the goals that lead toward it vary from year to year. So every single year, I make what I call my Best-Day-Ever Board; it's a collage that's made up of images of my goals (mostly cut from magazines) for that year. Not only is this a visual cue for me that reinforces my mission statement, but it also engages my family. I keep that board in a place of honor in our house, where I see it and my husband sees it and my children see it every single day. My kids ask questions about it, and my husband points to it when he sees me going off course. They all help me to remember how I'm going to live out my personal mission in the days and weeks and months ahead.

Another way you can reinforce your mission statement in your brain is to get up every morning and read it before you begin your day. Post it on your mirror, so you see it every day. A few years ago, I put both my personal mission statement on my mirror and Post-Its with words that connected to my mission—like "joy," "integrity," "connected," and "abundant." Every time I looked in the mirror, those words formed a halo around my reflection, forcing me to remember them each time I looked at my face. They helped me set my course for the day by reminding me how I wanted my day to feel and be.

Another strategy that's helped me to reconnect with my mission statement throughout the day is setting my phone alarm to ding three times a day with a positive word that pulls me back to my mission. This year, the words I've chosen are "vibrant," "authentic," and "connected." Each time I get pinged, I take a quick pause in my day, a moment when I simply breathe and ask myself if I'm embodying that word. When I see the word "connected," I ask myself: "Did I return the texts I got this morning? Did I answer that e-mail from a friend? Let me do that right now." When I see, "authentic," I know I need to be living my mission—and what that looks like right now might be something as simple as giving someone a smile or pausing to listen to a story around the water cooler. Then when the word "vibrant" pings me, I take a breath and ask myself: "How am I feeling right now? Am I feeling bright and full of life?" If I'm not, then I need to do something about it—take five deep breaths, go for a walk around the block, or whatever I need to do to restore my energy.

There are scientific, neurological reasons why visual cues work so well to keep us connected to our personal mission statements. Athletes have known for decades that picturing themselves winning will actually improve their performance on the field, and neurologists have found that the brain patterns activated when, for example, a weightlifter lifts heavy weights are activated nearly as much when the lifter only visualized lifting weights. By giving ourselves visual cues, we encourage ourselves to make mental pictures of the actions we are hoping to achieve. Visual cues also activate the reticular activating system (RAS) in our brains.

Imagine you're walking through a busy airport. You're surrounded by noise, but you're not paying attention to any of it—until you hear your name being announced over the loudspeaker. When that happens, your RAS kicks on. Basically, it tells you, "Pay attention! This information is important!" Or let's say someone tells you to look for white Audis. Before you started looking for this particular kind of car, you never noticed them on the road—but now that you're looking for them, suddenly white Audis are everywhere. In reality, there's not a greater number of white Audis than there were before—but now, your RAS is pointing them out to you.

Your RAS acts a little like a filter between your conscious mind and your subconscious. When we give our RAS a visual or verbal message—such as "Notice opportunities to be kind"—the RAS will then bring to our attention those opportunities throughout the day. It's not magic. Those opportunities were always there, but now your mind is paying attention to them. When we see our mission statements and goals in words and pictures, over and over, we give our subconscious brain an extra little boost that will help us live them. We train our brains to see opportunities to embody our values in our everyday lives.

BUSINESS APPLICATION

Writer Ernest Holmes said, *"Life is a mirror and will reflect back to the thinker what he thinks into it."* Business coaches recommend using the reticular activating system (RAS) to help you build a successful enterprise. You do this by creating a clear, focused picture of what you want your business to achieve, which allows your RAS to kick into gear. It acts like an antenna.

Let's say you're looking to find new market niches for your product. If you mentally focus on that question, your RAS will act a little like Google: It will automatically start sifting through all the input that comes into your brain, searching for possible "matches." As a result, you'll find new market ideas popping up everywhere. They'll come to you while you're reading the newspaper, talking with friends, or watching television. Your conscious mind is your goal setter and your unconscious mind is your goal getter.

The old adage of "Be careful what you wish for" is based precisely on this principle. Your reticular activating system is constantly looking for ways to make your unconscious desires a reality. The key is to funnel that system into something useful by being clear in your goals and letting your subconscious help you by noticing things you otherwise would have overlooked.

To make this work most effectively, focus on one thing at a time, rather than trying to do a bunch of "searches" all at once. Your brain has amazing powers—so put them to use!

 MAKE IT PERSONAL

In this exercise, you will be creating your own vision board. Try to get over the silly name or the "woo-woo" aspect of this. This is another way to visualize your goals and see them. It's like a much more vibrant list. To do this project, gather a large piece of poster board or a cork board to start. You'll need a stack of magazines, index cards, scissors, tape, pins, and/or a glue stick. You might also want to use markers and stickers—anything that appeals to your fancy.

Before you can create a vision board, give yourself a week or two to leaf through magazines and cut out images that speak to you (I save photos throughout the year or print them out from the Internet). Choose ones that line up with the goals you've set yourself for the year ahead. Write any quotes that especially speak to you on the index cards.

Now set aside some time alone, when you won't be interrupted. Put on music, light a candle. Alternatively, you could have a "vision board" party and invite a few friends over to create visions boards together. Have fun as you cut and pin and paste. You might want to add words to your images. It's your board—you can do whatever you want!

Two examples of my vision boards from past years.

INSPIRATION

Peter Shallard, a business psychologist and author, describes how having an overarching mission encompasses everything in your life:

When your life is driven by the over-arching sense of direction that (only) a mission creates, everything you do is part of it . . . . Every action you take contributes, in some way, to the direction and momentum of the journey you are on.

When you're on a mission in life, everything becomes relevant . . . . Taking time to eat food is critical—it nourishes you and fuels your mission's success . . . . Will a ninety-minute massage derail your workflow or reinvigorate your mind and body to contribute even more?

Spend time with your significant other to nourish your spirit. Let your kids inspire you to make a world that's better for them. To contribute 110% to your mission, you'll need to look after yourself . . . . It's all part of it.

You need to trust that, so long as you hold a deep intention to fulfill a significant mission, no single behavior will derail you from your path. In fact, everything you do will lead you inexorably closer to realizing your vision.

#13

EXAMINE YOUR LIFE TO DETERMINE WHAT NEEDS TO CHANGE

Make sure your values shape your habits— and not the other way around.

Once you understand that habits can change, you have the freedom— and the responsibility—to remake them. Once you understand that habits can be rebuilt . . . the only option left is to get to work.

—CHARLES DUHIGG

A woman I was talking to recently confessed that, rather than working at her current job, what she really wants to do in life is help people. "I need to feel as though I'm making a difference in the world. I'd love to volunteer at a nursing home—or maybe the hospital. Or a youth center."

"So why don't you?" I asked.

"Oh, I can't," she said. "I just don't have time."

"Run through a typical day for me," I suggested. "Tell me what you do."

It turned out that most of her days looked pretty much like this: She went to work at an office job where she spent most of her day sitting in front of a computer. She usually worked late, and she often brought work home with her. At night, she was too tired to do anything but collapse on her sofa and turn on the television, snacking on junk food while she watched. Before she went to bed every night, she always had a bowl of ice cream, because, she said, "I deserve to have at least one thing I look forward to all day." Then she'd do it all again the next day.

If you listened to this woman talk, you would hear that she really values things like kindness, helping others, making a difference in the world. But if you looked at her life, you wouldn't see those values present. You'd think her values were work, television, and junk food.

She's not unique. Despite our best intentions, we don't always live our lives in a way that aligns with our true values. When that happens, we feel as though we're missing something important in our lives. We instinctively know something is wrong, and that cognitive dissonance leads us to try to fill the hole—with a bowl of ice cream or TV.

But those things are never going to give meaning to our lives. Best-Day-Ever lives match up values and action. They're built, piece by piece, by aligning the things we choose to do with the values we hold most important. Does this mean you're never going to enjoy a bowl of ice cream or a mindless TV show? No. But it means those things do not become the steady diet of your life.

To make that happen, we must be willing to change. The woman whose life is too busy for anything but work, television, and junk food needs to reassess how she's spending her time. It doesn't mean it's all bad, but it does need refining to match up to her values. Maybe she needs a new job—but even more, she needs to consciously align her values with what she does every day. For example, even the most boring office job will provide opportunities for her to demonstrate kindness to others. She might begin looking for occasions to help someone—her colleagues, her neighbors, her family—in small ways. She also might find that if she did volunteer work one evening a week, it could energize her instead of making her more tired.

Living our values isn't always easy. Often, we've fallen into habits—deep ruts in the way we use our time—that lead in opposite directions from the "why" that would give more meaning to our lives. Mahatma Gandhi once said, "Your beliefs become your thoughts, your thoughts become your words, your words become your actions, your actions become your habits, your habits become your values, your values become your destiny."

Don't let habits choose your values for you. Think about what you believe is most important—and then be willing to change your life, routine, and habits so that the two match.

BUSINESS APPLICATION

Business coach TW Walker, author of *Superhero Success*, recommends examining your current reality in order to identify the bad habits that are standing in your way. "If I have a result that I don't want," Walker says, "the first question I have to ask myself is how did I get there." The next step is to write down the habits you identify as leading you in the wrong direction—and then replace each with a new habit that will propel you forward rather than slow you down. "Once your goals become habits, everything starts to fall into place," he says.

Walker lists five habits he believes businesspeople often allow to block their success:

1. **Failure to delegate.** "You can't be everything to your business," says Walker, so trust others to do jobs that will pull you away from what you do best, allowing your company to run more smoothly, while you have more time to focus on the big picture instead of being caught up in micromanaging.

2. **Bottlenecking decision-making.** "Entrepreneurs like to have control," says Walker, but if every decision has to pass through you, then you'll slow down movement. People will be waiting for you to have time to make up your mind. Instead, consider setting a dollar limit on decisions that your employees can make without your input. This will be whatever your business can afford to lose should the decision be the wrong one, whether that's ten dollars or a hundred dollars or a thousand dollars. "Big" decisions that have the potential to have significant financial impact will still require your guidance, but little ones—like whether to buy a new coffee machine, for example, or invest in

another printer for the office—probably don't need your leadership.

3. **Being reactive instead of proactive.** "Strategic thinking is what you need in order to have the right habits," says Walker. When you have a clear idea about what's most important to you and your business (see Strategy #11), then you can create habits that lead you more directly to your goals, rather than slowing you down.

4. **Engaging in unproductive activities.** You may think you're "being productive and multitasking where in reality I believe that the whole idea of multitasking is unproductive," Walker says. Don't allow e-mail and social media to distract you from focused work.

5. **Fear.** "Fear actually takes time," Walker says. While you're worrying, you're not being creative. You're taking time away from important actions that will propel your business toward success.

 MAKE IT PERSONAL

- The Wheel of Life is a useful tool for examining how well your values and your life match up with each other. It divides life up into "pie pieces"—and your job now is to shade in the circle, on a scale of 1 to 10, indicating how satisfied you are with the amount of time you're spending on that area of your life. The values you identified in

Strategy #11 should have application to all these pie pieces, in one way or another.

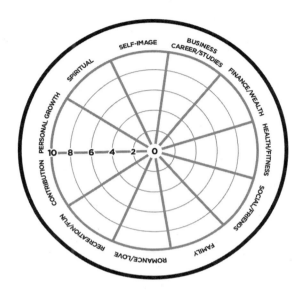

Once you've finished shading in your wheel, look at it. How balanced is it? If this were an actual wheel, would it be able to roll smoothly—or would it bump and jolt along because one or more sides are flat? What areas need more time than what you're currently giving them?

- Next, ask yourself: How can I improve in these areas? What can I do to make time to "round out" the areas of my life that are currently not what I want them to be? What things in my life could I drop—or at least curtail—so that I could fit in more of the things I *really* value? After writing your answers down, pick one thing to start doing differently this week.

INSPIRATION

Parker Palmer started his professional life as an advertising man in the *Mad Men* era. From the outside, his values appeared to be fast cars and the "large toys" by which men in the 1960s defined their selfhood. And then one day, he woke up to a sudden realization: "The life I am living is not the same as the life that wants to live in me."

Parker's values and his life were not aligned. And the success he gained in the outside world didn't *feel* like success, because it didn't match up with what was truly most important to him.

At first, he set out to live up to the loftiest, noblest ideals he could think of. But that didn't work either. Instead of listening to his own heart to hear his own "why," he was trying to impose on himself other people's values. In his book *Let Your Life Speak,* he wrote that his attempt to change his life "led me to conjure up the highest values I could imagine and then try to conform my life to them whether they were mine or not. If that sounds like what we are supposed to do with values, it is because that is what we are too often taught. There is a simplistic brand of moralism among us that wants to reduce the ethical life to making a list, checking it twice—against the index in some best-selling book of virtues, perhaps—and then trying very hard to be not naughty but nice."

Parker Palmer's experience is also a reminder that values must be personal. They must be *yours,* not someone else's. His advice: "Before you tell your life what truths and values you have decided to live up to, let your life tell you what truths you embody, what values you represent."

#14

ENLIST OTHERS
WHEN YOU PLAN

If the people in your life know the plan, then they can support it.

Let's say your goal for this year is to be able to run a half-marathon. It's something you've always wanted to do, and you know it's a good way to improve your physical fitness, which will allow you to be more effective in all the other areas of your life—but you feel a little embarrassed telling your friends and family that you've set for yourself such an ambitious goal. So you decide to keep it to yourself.

You've always enjoyed running, but now you know you're going to have to run at least three times a week, faithfully, rain or shine. You decide that the best way to fit in the running is early in the morning, before you go to work. So the first day, you set your alarm clock forty-five minutes earlier than usual, and the next morning you get up, stretch, and run for thirty minutes. You feel great all day, both physically and emotionally. The goal you've set for yourself excites you and gives you energy that gets you up and out the door two more times that week.

On Saturday, though, when you've planned your long run, your husband has other plans. "Let's go out to breakfast," he says.

"Let me do my run first," you tell him.

"Do it later," he says. "Come on, let's go to breakfast."

Later will work just as well, you tell yourself, and you go out for a leisurely breakfast. After eating a stack of pancakes, though, you're too stuffed to think about running—and by the time you've got your energy back, a friend has dropped by and wants to talk. Pretty soon, the entire day has gone by, and you've never managed to find time to run. "Oh well," you tell yourself, "I'll do it tomorrow."

But Sunday morning you sleep late—"I deserve to have one day a week that I sleep in," you tell yourself—and then you have to go to your parents for dinner and your kids need help with their homework, and now yet another day has gone by.

You're determined to get up Monday morning and run—and you do, but then your husband needs you to take the kids to school for the rest of the week, and you can't seem to find time in your mornings, even though you get up early. "Maybe I should switch my run to after work," you tell yourself. So you try that—but there are even more demands on your time from your family during your evenings.

Pretty soon a month has gone by, and you realize you're never going to be able to train in time for the race. "Maybe next year," you tell yourself, and you let that particular goal drop out of your mind.

Think how different things might have been if you had told your husband, your children, and close friends the goal you had set yourself. Not only could they have helped to hold you accountable to your running schedule, but they also could have actively cooperated in helping you find the time to run every morning. Their excitement and pride in your accomplishment would have motivated you even more to succeed. When my husband was training for his first marathon, the kids and I often joined him as a family. When I was training for my half-marathon, he would load the kids up in the car and meet me at places along the training run to cheer me on and buoy my spirits.

Whenever we set ourselves a goal, we need to consider that it will affect the other people in our lives. None of us live in a bubble, so our plans intersect with the lives of our family, colleagues, and friends. We need their input as we make our plans. If we include them from the very beginning of the process, we can enlist their help in achieving our Best Day Ever.

 BUSINESS APPLICATION

You can't have private business goals. You need to engage your entire team if you hope to achieve your goals. Author and speaker Verne Harnish calls this having a "theme," and he encourages businesses to design an annual theme to get all team members aligned with company goals. This needs to be done intentionally and deliberately, and then it needs to be monitored and managed. For example, one year Bramble Berry did a giant papier-mâché mountain (it was about five feet wide and three feet tall). We had different levels of climbers and different heights that correlated with goals. Once the team hit a goal, the climbers would scale the mountain to the point that corre-lated with that goal. It was a visual representation of how we were progressing on our goals.

Because people within your business need to be clear on exactly what your short- and long-term goals are, they need to be discussed and they also need to be measured. One year, our theme was "Around the World," so every team member was given a passport and different goals were worth different stamps. That year, we were working on reducing absenteeism and mistakes, so stamps were given out for those goals. Each day of passport stamps was worth an entry for someone to win a trip at the end of the year.

Designing thoughtful goals and explaining them helps team members understand how their daily work contributes to organizational success. They'll know that their work and efforts matter. Currently, we have an entire wall with metrics on it that everyone can see, so that visually, at a glance, staff will know how the company is doing in a variety of areas, from order turnaround to mistakes to employee efficiency per hour. The more pieces of informa-tion you share, the more pieces of the puzzle your smart and motivated team will have so they can feel connected to and aligned with the company's future. When you get everyone in the organization running in the same direction with both passion and purpose, you'll have a major piece of the business success puzzle in place.

MAKE IT PERSONAL

Before you commit to your yearly goals, sit down with your family and discuss your family schedule. With a daily calendar in front of you, write down your commitments as a family throughout the day; include everyone's activities. Then share with each other the goals you would each like to achieve in the year ahead.

Look to see how your goals will intersect. How much time will everyone need for their plans? What is the best time of day for them? If you can't see a slot where you can easily fit your plans, brainstorm with your family how you might find a compromise. Would another family member be able to shift something around to help you? What might you be willing to do in return, to help other family members achieve their goals? My kids are toddlers right now, so this process mostly takes place between my husband and me. I have been told by others that, as the kids get older, family meetings like this will become increasingly important.

INSPIRATION

While sharing your goals with family and close friends helps to create an accountability group of support, there may be a limit to how far and wide you want to spread your goals. At least, that's what some research has shown. Several psychology studies have found there is a downside to loudly and strongly proclaiming what your future achievements will be.

Why is this true? Because, per psychologist Peter Gollwitzer, telling a wide group of people your goals may give you the emotional satisfaction of accomplishing the goal without having to actually do the work. Talking can become a substitute for doing.

Dr. Gollwitzer conducted a study in 2009 where he asked 163 people to write down a small personal goal. Then half of them announced out loud their commitment to their goal; half of them didn't. They were all given forty-five minutes to work toward their goal but were told they could stop at any time.

Participants who had kept their goals to themselves worked the entire forty-five minutes and later reported they felt they still had more work to do to before accomplishing their goals. On the other hand, those who had gone public quit working after only thirty-three minutes on average; they felt they were already close to accomplishing their goals and didn't need to work the entire time.

If our goals affect others' lives, then it's important to enlist their help and cooperation and build a group of cheerleading supporters that will help you achieve your vision. Think twice, however, before pre-bragging too loudly and broadly about your goals—you don't want to be guilty of letting your *talking* replace your *doing*.

#15

PRACTICE ACCOUNTABILITY

Use practical tools to keep yourself aligned with your goals.

Accountability separates the wishers in life from the action-takers that care enough about their future to account for their daily actions.

—JOHN DI LEMME

When we set goals for ourselves, we don't want them to disappear into the ether. We want to keep track of them. Accountability helps us do that. It demands that we answer the question (if only to ourselves), "Did I follow through on this goal?"

Accountability makes us responsible for follow-through. It also helps us to measure our success and progress—and that helps to motivate us. Seeing successes accumulate feels good; it makes us want to work harder, and it keeps us engaged, so that we don't get distracted from our goals.

One common accountability strategy is to use an online or app-based service to place a bet. (At this writing, Stickk and Beeminder are two services for this.) If you don't do what you say you'll do, then the money goes to an organization you loathe. The idea here is to put some skin in the game and create a consequence that happens if you don't follow through.

Forming an accountability group is another tool I use whenever I'm working toward a goal that will take longer than a week or two. I especially use it for fitness and health. It can work a couple of different ways. Each member in the group might have individual goals. Someone might want to lose ten pounds, another might want to learn to dance the rumba, and another wants to start a daily workout program. When the group gets together, each member reports on how well she's been sticking to her goal. Another way to do an accountability group is to pull together a group of people who are all working toward the same goal. For example, I recently led a group of women through a sugar-detox nutritional plan. We were in contact every single day via social media, reporting what we'd eaten, what our struggles were, how we were feeling, and what we'd found helpful. In both kinds of accountability groups, the members of the group hold each other accountable. They inspire each other and encourage each other.

When I was getting my master's degree, I was also working at Bramble Berry full time, so I couldn't just decide to take a few days off and study. This meant I had to study in the mornings—and I knew that was going to take discipline. To keep myself accountable, I enlisted the help of a very successful entrepreneur. He agreed to take a phone call message from me every morning at 5:30, when I was getting up to study. So every morning at 5:30, I left him a message that said, "Hey. I'm up. I'm studying." This entrepreneur's success represented something I very much wanted to imitate, and he was someone I respected and admired. Because I didn't want to let him down or disappoint him, I was motivated to show him my commitment to studying. I never missed a phone call, and his willingness to be my accountability partner helped catapult me far past what I originally thought I could achieve.

When you work with others, either in a group or one-to-one, accountability almost always works out to be a two-way street. It's something we do for each other, to help us go further than we could go alone. This means it's not about competition; it's not a question of who can achieve more or of judging someone who stumbles. Instead, accountability is about helping all of us truly live our Best Day Ever, every day.

 BUSINESS APPLICATION

Linda Galindo, author of *The 85% Solution: How Personal Accountability Guarantees Success*, says accountability partners are an entrepreneur's secret weapon for quick growth. She offers four tips for finding a good match and making the most of the relationship:

1. **Look outside of your industry.** Someone outside your field may be able to offer fresh ideas about your industry.

2. **Choose someone who will be (brutally) honest with you.** "You're not looking for someone who will rescue, fix or save you," Galindo says. She

also says that for your partner to be able to do this, you should look for someone who has qualities you lack.

3. **Be clear about your expectations.** Decide how often you will communicate and whether it will be in person, over the phone, or by e-mail. Set limits on how many projects and commitments you'll discuss at a time. Be clear that whether or not you take your partner's advice, each of you is totally responsible for your own choices.

4. **Agree on consequences.** Galindo believes accountability partners must hold each other to consequences if commitments go uncompleted. Whether there is a financial risk (for example, "You owe me a hundred dollars if you don't complete your goal") or something more fun and informal ("I'll take you out to dinner at the restaurant of your choice if I don't follow through with my goal"), consequences give greater urgency to accountability. When I have mentees, I'll often impose a financial penalty that is personally meaningful as a negative incentive for missing a goal. For example, a large donation to a politician or a cause they particularly dislike or strongly disagree with is usually a surefire way to get procrastinators to finish up major projects or start their goals strong.

MAKE IT PERSONAL

Working on accountability with a group or an individual is an effective way to keep our goals on track, but you can also practice accountability alone. How do you do that? Here are some of my favorite methods:

- I use a large paper calendar to check off whether I did or didn't follow through on my goals each day. That paper record keeps me accountable.

- If you like tech-based options, use one of the many apps available to track your goals. There are many (with more coming out monthly), including Nozbe, GoalsOnTrack, LifeTick, Strides, and Coach.Me. Some of these build in crowdsourced feedback as an enhanced form of personal accountability.

Your assignment? Research the apps that are available. If one of them appeals to you, start using it tomorrow. If not, get yourself a planner or calendar, and keep track of your goals there. Don't rely on your memory to hold you accountable, because memories can play tricks, convincing us that we're doing far better than we actually are. You need a visible record to keep you accountable to the goals that will help you fulfill your mission in life.

INSPIRATION

Leigh Stringer, author of *The Healthy Workplace*, writes about the power of peer pressure to help us achieve goals. "I noticed," she says, "that some of the really healthy, outcome-focused organizations I visited during my research were using these peer-based partnerships to help their employees meet not only personal health goals but also business goals. It turns out this peer pressure thing, when you turn up the 'accountability' knob, is a motivator for a lot more than losing a few pounds. Compared to mentorship—a more hierarchical relationship— a peer-to-peer relationship seems to be easier to organize, and it is a more effective tool for making progress toward a goal. Accountability partnerships work when they are a collaboration between two colleagues who like and respect one another—your partner is someone you trust who will keep you honest and moving on a path you set for yourself."

Stringer recommends these steps for setting up an accountability partnership:

- Find someone you trust to be your accountability partner (a different personality from you is good, maybe better).
- Talk to that person about your goals.

- Get specific about actions you will want to take to meet your goals as well as consequences/rewards for taking or not taking them.

- Set up regular check-in times. (This can be a text message; there's no need to meet every time.)

- Revisit goals and strategies periodically to make sure you are on track.

#16

LIVE IN THE NOW, PLAN FOR THE FUTURE

Appropriate planning means you'll have the resources you need down the road.

Planning is bringing the future into the present so that you can do something about it now.

—ALAN LAKEIN

I have deliberately structured my life around my passion—inspiring people to be creative in the ways they improve their lives every day. This means that "now" is all about nurturing and expressing that passion. I don't have to wait for some moment in the future to begin living it.

This means that sometimes I have to do things today that aren't necessarily joyful in order to make sure I'll have the resources I need to continue living my passion in the future. Take paying the bills, for example. I have a stack of checks on my desk that need to be signed. Do I find joy in auditing those checks and making sure they're written to the right places for the right amounts? Nope. There's no joy in accounting for me (but I'm happy that other people love it). It's a practice that needs to be done today, though, if I want to continue to be in business for the long term.

Living in the now must incorporate a long-term strategy. This is like Strategy #6—use a long-term perspective because everything you do has countless tiny reverberations—but this strategy focuses on actual *planning*: laying out the actions you'll take now to ensure that you'll have what you need to carry out your goals.

Here are some of my most distant long-term goals: I want to live a long and healthy life. I want to be vibrant at the age of eighty-five. I want to still be mobile at the age of ninety-five. I want to see my kids graduate from college, get married, and have their own children. I want to feel joy every day, no matter how old I am. To achieve all those goals, I must make a plan today that is built on the right choices.

My daily plan includes fueling my body with the right foods, so I'll have the joy and energy I need to live my Best Day Ever for the rest of my life. I have an exercise plan for the same reason. I don't make these plans because I love saying no to Snickers bars or because I'm thrilled to get up an extra half hour early to exercise. When that Snickers bar is tempting me or my alarm is ringing, it always seems like it would be a lot more fun to gobble up the candy or sleep a little longer. But I know the chocolate and caramel that taste so good in my mouth will give me sugar lows later in the day, and enough of them will make me gain weight, which would make me cranky in all sorts of ways. I also love the way I feel later in the day when I've exercised in the morning. All this means that

I'm powerfully motivated to follow through on my plans. I don't have exercise and nutrition plans because I *should,* and they're not something I do because I'm such a good and righteous person; I have them because they help me feel the way I want to feel for the rest of my life.

The same principle applies to having a plan for my money (otherwise known as a budget) and my time (a schedule). I want to be sure that I'll be able to do the things I want later in the month, as well as next year—and ten or twenty years from now.

To get a better grasp on this strategy, think about what it takes for a city to prepare for an earthquake. The earthquake could happen at any time—today, next year, twenty years from now—so constructing quake-resilient buildings, bridges, and roads can't be postponed. It's a long-term plan that starts right now. Or consider the US Constitution; it was written to meet the needs of a young nation, with the understanding that it could also be an ongoing roadmap that would endure for the centuries ahead. We each need our personal versions of plans like these.

As I described back in Strategy #11, A Deeper Dive: A Good Mission Statement Focuses Your Plans, I have regular personal planning sessions to make sure my long-term goals fit into my day-to-day schedule. My week-by-week plan wouldn't be possible, however, if I couldn't match it up with big goals for the entire year. In our family, my husband and I have an annual meeting to plan out our year. First, we come up with our individual goals, and then we check in with each other to come up with our shared family goals. It's important that we work on our goals together, so our individual goals and overall family goals don't conflict. Personally, I start coming up with a rough draft in November for the following year's goals, instead of waiting for the end of December. The thankfulness I feel during

November makes a good foundation for goal setting, and there's more time for reflection than I usually have amid the busyness of the December holiday season.

Your own yearly goals might include adding more exercise or furthering your education. A family goal could be something like spending one weekend a month doing something with your kids that is fun, interesting, and out of the ordinary. Another family goal might be answering the question: "How much are we going to save this year?"

By the beginning of the New Year, my goals are finalized. Then, throughout the year, I check in with those goals. I take about an hour once a month to look back at the previous month and plan the one ahead to stay on target. I pay attention to what worked in last month's plan—and what didn't work. Then I write down what I will change this month. Based on that, I create my schedule for the month ahead to keep on track. Every Sunday night, I sit down with my schedule and goals to make sure I'm still on target. I figure out what I can do that week to move myself forward a little more. It sounds like a lot, but it's just a habit-based rhythm. You get used to it; you even get addicted to it when you see the progress you're making.

I do the same sort of thing at work, involving my team in setting yearly goals and making plans. We have "daily huddles," where we run through a quick plan for our day, with yearly and quarterly goals forming the foundation for those day-by-day choices.

Living your Best Day Ever will always mean straddling the present moment and the future through thoughtful planning, so that down the road you have everything you need.

BUSINESS APPLICATION

Small-business journalist Jennifer Williams offers these examples of long-term business goals and the short-term goals that will lead to them:

Revenue

Long-term:

- Double revenue by the end of the current fiscal year.

Short-term:

- Contract an advertising consultant for one month to help you analyze and capitalize on your customers' buying trends.

- Spend the next month learning your primary competition and brainstorming on what you offer that they don't.

- Take this research and design a new advertising campaign that highlights the unique points about your business or products.

Customer Service

Long-term:

- Receive at least 95 percent positive customer feedback regarding the service you provide.

Short-term:

- Redesign the customer service research process to include new questionnaires and incentives, such as monthly drawings for free products or discounts on future purchases for customers who take the time to respond.

Employee Appreciation

Long-term:

- Award an employee-of-the-year award to the employee who provides the most creative input during the year in terms of practical ideas to improve the company.

Short-term:

- Award employee-of-the-month throughout the year to mark the progression of creative input, and to include more employees in the reward process.

Community Outreach

Long-term:

- Build the company's name recognition within the community through community outreach projects.

Short-term:

- Reward employees who volunteer with designated community programs with additional time off, bonuses, or gift cards.
- Choose one or two high-profile annual charity events to sponsor.

Website Traffic

Long-term:

- Increase traffic to your company's website by at least 50 percent by the end of the current year.

Short-term:

- Research and purchase Web traffic analysis software to better pinpoint current traffic trends.

- Hire a web consultant for one month to propose and implement programming changes to make the site appeal to a broader audience.

- Select a medium for advertising your site other than the web, such as a bus campaign where you advertise your site address on the side of city buses for one month, or billboards, where you lease a billboard in a conspicuous place in town for one month.

 MAKE IT PERSONAL

Masters of long-term planning have a variety of strategies that merge the journey with the destination. Researchers Thomas Bateman and Bruce Berry found eight key strategies for motivating long-term planning:

1. **Allegory**: Comparing yourself to other inspiring stories, either from literature or real life. ("I am like Odysseus on a voyage of discovery." "I am following in the footsteps of Madame Curie.")

2. **Futurity**: Focusing on the long-term impact and possibilities associated with the ultimate outcomes of your goal. ("I will live longer because of the choices I make today." "I am building a better world for my children.")

3. **Self**: Making statements that emphasize your identity and personal belief systems. ("I am doing this because I am a creative person who needs to express herself." "This is important to my identity as a compassionate person.")

4. **Singularity**: Identifying what is unique about what you're doing. ("I will be the first person in my family to finish college." "No other woman has accomplished this before.")

5. **Knowledge**: Emphasizing how your work will generate new understanding and truths. ("No matter what happens, I will have learned so much by doing this." "I will gain insights I can teach to others, improving their lives as well as my own.")

6. **The Work**: Thinking about the nature of the work, including challenges, risks, and uncertainties, as well as elements that are fun or surprising. ("It's like solving a puzzle." "It's like an adventure story.")

7. **Embeddedness**: Looking at how this long-term goal will increase your value within your social context. ("I'm going to prove my family wrong when they said I couldn't do it." "I will earn my friends' respect.")

8. **Progress**: Finding short-term evidence that you're moving closer to your long-term goal. ("When I finish this semester, I will be that much closer to getting my master's degree."

"When I write this chapter, I will have reached the halfway point in my book.")

Create your own statements for a few of these strategies to help motivate your long-term plans.

If you haven't done the exercise in Strategy #11's Deeper Dive, you may want to go back and combine that exercise with this one. Once you know what your goals for the year ahead are, set aside an hour to plan the month ahead, using those goals as your guidelines. Break the month down week by week, and then day by day.

Remember, there will always be things in our schedules that may not seem directly related to our goals—things like going to the dry cleaner's, paying bills, changing the car's oil, or meeting with an accountant—but if you think about it, you'll be able to see that even these small, boring tasks in one way or another are necessary for you to reach your goals. Don't leave them out of your plan!

After a week, take at least half an hour to look back and see how well you did at keeping to your plan. Then answer these questions:

- What did you get accomplished this week that you probably wouldn't have if you hadn't planned ahead?

- What *didn't* you get accomplished this week that you had hoped to do?

- Why weren't you able to do these things? For example, were your plans for the week unrealistic? Did something unexpected come up that interfered with your plans?

Repeat this process each week. Don't get discouraged if at first you have difficulty sticking to your plans. Simply writing down your plans, along with your successes and failures, will make you more conscious of the need to integrate long-term plans into your life. Like everything else, the more you practice, the easier it becomes—until eventually it turns into a habit.

 INSPIRATION

Imagine you are a member of the team involved with NASA's New Horizons project to take close-up photos of Pluto. You'd probably be excited to be part of a never-done-before opportunity, one with the potential to bring new knowledge to the human race. But would you be able to hold on to your excitement and dedication during the five years needed to build the spacecraft and prepare for launch? And if so, would you *still* be able to keep committed to the project during the nearly ten years the spacecraft took to navigate its way across the solar system?

 You might think it takes a special kind of person to be part of such a long-term project. Researchers, however, have found that being good at a job requiring long-term plans isn't so much about patience and being naturally good at waiting. It depends much more on finding sources of motivation in the present you're living as well as the future you're envisioning—and motivation is the result of creating both short- and long-term plans. Discipline is another necessary component of any successful long-term plan. (Re-read Strategy #3!)

#17

BE REALISTIC

Set doable daily priorities.

Prioritize your passion. It keeps you sane.

—CRISS JAMI

If you've been doing the exercises in this book as you read, you have your yearly goals. They're broken down into quarters and months, and you've established processes for monthly and weekly planning. The next step is to break down your plans into daily priorities.

I have only one to three priorities on any single day. That's it. The temptation is always to give ourselves a whole bunch of daily priorities. The act of writing our long list of ten or more items feels as though we've already accomplished something great. In fact, the longer your list, the less likely you are to achieve the items on it. You'll be able to use the power of the trudge (see A Deeper Dive in Strategy #5) when you focus on small, achievable steps each day.

We also have the tendency to plan for an ideal day, where there are no interruptions, no unplanned events, no emergencies. How many days do we actually have like that during a week? One or two at most, if we're really lucky. So don't give yourself more than three priorities to accomplish in a day. That way you'll be setting yourself up for success rather than failure and frustration.

You can (of course) have a whole bunch of little things on your to-do list, but out of those, choose only one to three things that must get done before the end of the day. It's about prioritizing, not flooding. Then try to check them off before noon. Get them done before your brain is tired—and before anything else demands your attention and knocks you off course.

There's a story that's been floating around for a while that illustrates this concept. It goes something like this: A professor began class one day by setting an empty jar on his desk and then filling it to the top with rocks. Then he turned to the class and asked, "Is the jar full?"

They agreed that it was. But then the professor poured a bag of pebbles slowly into the jar, shaking the jar a little while he did so. The pebbles rolled into the open areas between the rocks, and the entire bag fit into the jar. "Now is the jar full?" the professor asked the class.

They laughed and agreed that now the jar was truly full. The professor then picked up a bag of sand and slowly poured it into the jar. As the sand sifted down through the cracks between the rocks and pebbles, the professor was able to pour the entire bag into the jar.

"Now," said the professor to his students, "if I tell you that this little exercise illustrates something about your life, can you tell me what that is?"

"If you try harder, you can do more," said one student.

"There is always a way to fit more into your schedule," said another.

"We have all the time we need to get things done," said a third.

The professor proceeded to dump the entire contents of the jar out onto his desk. Then he asked the class, "If I told you to put this mess back into the jar, would you be able to do it?"

After a moment, one student said, "Only if we put the stones in first, then the pebbles, and finally the sand. Otherwise it won't all fit."

"Exactly," said the professor. "And your lives are the same. If you don't put the big rocks—the things that are most important—into your life first, you won't have time for them in your life. But when you do them first, then you'll be able to fit in smaller things around them once they're done. Do you understand?"

The students nodded their heads. "Keep in mind," said the professor, "that the 'sand' in your lives are the trivial things in life—like texting, Facebook, Instagram, watching television. If you put these things into your life first, you'll never have all the time you need for other more important things. If you put them in last, though, they can fill up the small extra spaces in your time."

The moral of the story is clear: Creating a daily plan based initially on a few main priorities allows you to fit even more into your life later. It puts you in control of your time, and it enables you to shape the life you want to lead!

 BUSINESS APPLICATION

Setting priorities in the business world is essential. Here are two points to keep in mind:

Priorities must be realistic and time appropriate. If you say, "My priority for my workday is to read all the new research on this particular topic," that may be unproductive. It's not that you shouldn't do your research, but you might benefit more from completing concrete projects rather than reading literature at work.

Attend to your daily priorities before you check your e-mail. E-mail is a necessary part of the day—but it can also be an enormous time waster. You could be sitting all day staring at your computer screen, doing nothing but reading and answering e-mail. Responding to e-mails all day long is a reactive rather than proactive way to handle your life; you're constantly responding to others instead of having control over your own time.

There's an old saying: "If the first thing you do when you wake up each morning is eat a live frog, nothing worse can happen for the rest of the day." That's probably true. Author Brian Tracey has said that your frog should be the most difficult task on your to-do list; the one you're most likely to pro-crastinate on. Because if you accomplish that first, it will give you energy and momentum for the rest of the day. If you don't and you let it sit there while you do other unimportant things, it can drain your energy. William James, a famous psychologist said, "Procrastination is attitude's natural assassin. There is nothing so fatiguing as an uncompleted task."

 MAKE IT PERSONAL

- List one to three priorities for each day this week. Each of these "trudge steps" should connect specifically and directly to your larger long-term goals. Commit to getting these smaller tasks accomplished no matter how long the rest of your to-do list is for that day. For example, this might be writing a proposal for a client, pricing out a product line, or pitching a product to stores. All of these are key behaviors to get you to your final destination, even if they're not particularly fun, easy, or creative. Avoid the temptation to put them off to do another day.

- List some of the activities in your life you should consider "sand" to be fit in after other more important things are done.

- At the end of the week, look back and assess what you accomplished. Did you get more or less accomplished this week than usual? Were you able to distinguish between the rocks, pebbles, and sand in your life?

 INSPIRATION

Stephen Covey had many helpful things to say about setting priorities. Here are several of his most inspiring comments on this topic:

"The key is not to prioritize what's on your schedule, but to schedule your priorities."

(For example, this could mean putting gym time on your schedule and treating it like an appointment.)

"The main thing is to keep the main thing the main thing."

(For example, this could mean that if your reason for being is your family, then schedule Family Nights weekly.)

"Most of us spend too much time on what is urgent and not enough time on what is important."

(For example, this might mean not letting daily distractions of e-mails derail us from our big tasks for the week or the month.)

"You have to decide what your highest priorities are and have the courage—pleasantly, smilingly, non-apologetically, to say 'no' to other things. And the way you do that is by having a bigger 'yes' burning inside. The enemy of the 'best' is often the 'good.'"

(For example, this could be saying no to the things that do not get you to your larger goal of a happy family, healthy physical well-being, or the degree you are working on.)

Manage your Resources

PART III

Manage Your Resources!

Use time, money, and your physical strength effectively.

#18

WHAT IS MEASURED CAN BE IMPROVED

Find out where your time is currently spent—and make changes.

Measurement is the first step that leads to control

and eventually to improvement.

If you can't measure something, you can't understand it.

If you can't understand it, you can't control it.

If you can't control it, you can't improve it.

—**H. JAMES HARRINGTON**

Time may be our greatest resource, the gift that's given to each of us to use to improve our lives and the world around us. The good news is—we're all given the same amount of time each day. It's as though every time we wake up, someone hands us a $1,000 check and says, "Here. Use this however you want today. And tomorrow you'll get another one just like this." It's better than collecting $200 every time you pass GO in Monopoly!

Despite this generous ongoing gift, we often complain that we never have the time we need. In fact, if time were actually money, we'd feel like we were living in poverty.

How can that be when we're each given the same amount of time every day? How come some people seem to do so much with that daily gift, while others struggle to get the bare minimum accomplished? It's *not* because some of us are better people, just naturally faster or more efficient at doing things. Instead, it has to do with the choices we make about how to use our time each day.

One of my accountability groups (see Strategy #15 – Practice Accountability) recently read the book *The Compound Effect,* by Darren Hardy. In the book, Hardy talks about the importance of measuring your time to ensure you're spending it on the right things. A woman in our group tracked her time for an entire month and then reported back that she had become more aware of where she was wasting time in her day. I decided to try it.

First I tried paper and pen, and wow, that did not work. I forgot the notebook or I couldn't find a pen. That low-tech method was not consistent enough for my needs. Then I tried different time-tracker apps for my iPhone, since I'm rarely without my phone. The time tracker app I liked the best is Eternity. They offer a free trial version I tried, and then I quickly upgraded to the paid version when I realized the app could do everything I wanted. Once I set up my categories (this took about thirty minutes), I religiously started tracking my time.

At first, tracking my time seemed to take away from my ability to be in the present, aware of the "now," especially with my family. I had to physically remove myself from whatever situation I was in to pick up my phone and switch on my task. I worked through that quickly by making a switch where it really mattered: I made sure that "family" was just one main category without any subcategories. That kept the phone out of my hand as much as possible when I was with my kids. I did design categories for "play," however, to ensure that I was measuring how much time I worked out, saw my friends, and did date night with my sweet husband—but I kept them to a minimum so I could be in the moment whenever I was having valuable relationship time.

THIS IS MY WORK LIFE BROKEN DOWN INTO MAJOR CATEGORIES FOR ONE MONTH:

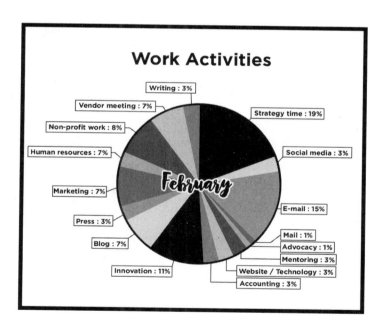

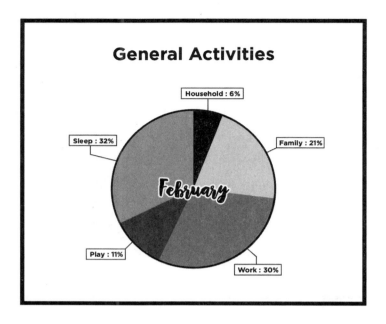

I learned some interesting things. First, e-mail is the black hole of time wasting. When I first started time tracking, I was horrified when I saw how much time I was spending on e-mail: 25 percent of my work time! Talk about not being productive!

Second, I could *really* see how well I was spending my time in relation to the goals I had set myself. If I was spending huge chunks of time on something that moved me no closer to any of my goals, then I obviously needed to rethink the way I was using that time. If time is a resource, then we want to be sure we're spending it on what's really most important to us—not letting it trickle away on small silly things.

The principle is pretty much the same as having a budget. If you think you're saving for a family vacation, but you're actually spending all your money on daily tiny impulse buys . . . well, you have a problem, and you're unlikely to reach your goal. Until you start tracking where your money is going, it trickles away, just like time does. As Darren Hardy points out, "The real cost of a four-dollar-a-day coffee habit over 20 years is $51,833.79. That's the power of the Compound Effect."

Third, tracking my time helped me realize where I've been over-promising and under-delivering. This was especially clear in my professional life. If new ventures are going to be successful, then they need more of my time than older ones do, but I hadn't been giving them the attention they needed. Now I could see what needed to change. What gets measured can be fixed!

Fourth, I realized that anything that can be measured can be delegated. Obviously, we don't want to delegate our time with our family to someone else—but in our professional lives, it's entirely possible that someone else could be doing some of the things that consume so much of our time. My rule is simple: If it takes me more than five minutes and someone else *can* do it, then I delegate. I am trying to grow the "strategy," "marketing," and "mentoring" slices of my work pie graph, because those are the things that will help get my company to the next level by improving my team and how we communicate. By measuring my time and observing whether my high-level activities pie sections are growing larger (because I'm spending more time on them), I can tell if I'm doing a good job outsourcing and delegating—or if I've fallen into the trap of "it's easier to do it myself." While it may be easier for me to do some tasks than it is for others to tackle them, it doesn't mean that it is necessarily the best use of my time.

Not every slice in your time pie chart can be significantly changed. For example, making sure your family has clean underwear is pretty much a nonnegotiable element of family life that will always need to be accomplished—and you're probably not lingering over the job, wasting your time putting each undergarment into the machine one at a time. But measurement allows you to spot areas that *can* be changed—so that you have more time to live your Best Day Ever.

 ## BUSINESS APPLICATION

You may be convinced that tracking your time is a useful time-management strategy—but what if you're so sold on the idea that you'd like to have your team track *their* time? It's always tempting when you've found something that works beautifully for you to shout it from the rooftops and encourage others to do it. If you decide to do this at your workplace, tread carefully.

There's a good chance that, when you first introduce the idea to your team members, some of them will not be happy about it. They may feel that you do not trust them or that you are trying to catch them doing something wrong. In order to be fully engaged and committed to tracking their time, they need to see how it will *personally* benefit them by helping them streamline their work and make it more efficient. If the 80/20 rule applies to time management, 80 percent of the valuable work in a day gets done in 20 percent of the time. Wouldn't it be great if your team knew what the most valuable 20 percent of tasks were in a given day and then prioritized those? Think of how much productivity and job success people would feel if they could hit an extra goal per year.

One practical side to everyone on the team tracking their time is that it can help your business set more realistic pricing for its product or services, while at the same keeping expenses down, thus increasing profit margins—which is ultimately better for everyone at your company.

 MAKE IT PERSONAL

Before you commit to tracking your time for a month (or a year), I suggest you try it for a week. Use whatever time-tracking tool works best for you—a paper calendar, a notebook, an app on your phone, an online calendar—and commit to keeping a running tally under these main categories: family, fun, work, personal. You'll then need to make your own subcategories under each of those headings. Make it detailed enough to be useful, but not so detailed that you'll never be able to do it. At the end of the week, add up the hours you spend under each of the four large categories, and create your own pie graphs.

- When you look at your pie graphs, does the size of any of the "slices" surprise you? If so, which ones?

- Are there areas of your life that are consuming more time than you want, taking away from time that could help you reach your goals? If so, which ones?

- Are there other areas that aren't getting enough of your time, areas that would lead you closer to your goals—and if so, which ones?

- Did this exercise help you feel you have more power over your life and your time? What did you learn?

Set yourself new time targets for next week. Remember, you can't add time to one area without taking time away from something else! To see if you're successful, you'll need to spend another week measuring your time. At the end of that time, consider making new pie charts to give yourself a visual representation of where you've been successful in matching your time to your goals—and where you need further work.

 INSPIRATION

What can be measured can be improved—and then measuring your improvement also provides motivation to keep going. That's what Nike discovered when they started using their shoes to track athletes' performance.

At first Nike was simply interested in using the data to build better shoes. But then, as the Nike team noticed athletes' reactions, they realized that this could be an amazing tool to share with everyone. Through its partnership with Apple and its Nike+

platform, Nike put sensors in shoes that allowed activity to be measured—and then show up on smartphones, laptops, and online conversations with friends and fellow runners. Runners were thrilled—and they were motivated to run faster and longer.

The Nike+ FuelBand was Nike's next push toward keeping us motivated to exercise. Its rubberized wristband has sensors that measure the steps you take, the calories you burn, and something they call "Fuel points." That way you can compare running to swimming, say—or playing tennis to walking the dog, or dancing to skiing.

"It's a way for people to set simple, daily goals," Stefan Olander, VP Digital Sport at Nike, told *Wired* magazine. "You don't make it this massive change. You have to think about it as the least amount of uncomfortable change. We don't say, go out and run a marathon tomorrow, it's this incremental change. There is this nudge to keep you going."

Fuel points measure oxygen consumption during exercise, which is why they apply no matter what activity you're engaged in. "You want to have something to compare and compete over, whatever your sport or activity is," Olander said.

Nike Fuelbands may no longer be the most popular brand out there for measuring fitness goals—but they innovated and showed us how motivating measuring could be. What is measurable is changeable.

A DEEPER DIVE: THE BEST TIME-MANAGEMENT STRATEGY IS THE ONE YOU'LL USE

Use time-management tools to help you achieve your goals.

He who every morning plans the transaction of the day
and follows out that plan, carries a thread
that will guide him through the maze of the most busy life.
But where no plan is laid, where the disposal of time
is surrendered merely to the chance of incidence, chaos will soon reign.

—VICTOR HUGO

When you think about what you need to stay on track with your goals, what's the first thing that comes to mind? A lot of people would say, "I need to get motivated." After reading Strategy #3 (You Can't Divorce Success from Discipline), you might say, "I need more discipline." It turns out, though, that researchers have found that neither motivation nor discipline are the determining factors that make some people follow through on their goals while others don't.

In a study published in the *British Journal of Health Psychology*, researchers measured how frequently people exercised over a two-week period when given exercise as a goal. First, the researchers randomly assigned 248 adults to one of three groups. Group 1 was the control group, who was asked to keep track of how frequently they exercised over the next two weeks. Before they left, each person was asked to read the opening three paragraphs of an unrelated novel. Group 2 was the motivation group, who was also asked to keep track of how frequently they exercised over the next two weeks. Then, each person was asked to read a pamphlet on the benefits of exercise for reducing the risk of heart disease. Participants in Group 2 were also told, "People who have stuck to a regular exercise program have found it to be very effective in reducing their chances of developing coronary heart disease." Group 3 was the intention group. To ensure that Groups 2 and 3 were equally motivated, Group 3 also read the motivational pamphlet and got the same speech as Group 2. Then Group 3 was also asked to explicitly state their intention to exercise by completing the following statement: "During the next week, I will partake in at least twenty minutes of vigorous exercise on [DAY] at [TIME OF DAY] at/in [PLACE]." After receiving these instructions, all three groups went on their way.

Two weeks later, here's what the researchers found: In the control group, 38 percent of participants exercised at least once per week. In the motivation group, 35 percent of participants exercised at least once per week. But in the intention group, 91 percent of participants exercised at least once per week! Simply by writing down a plan that said exactly when and where they intended to exercise, the participants in Group 3 were much more likely to follow through.

It turns out that the thing that pulls out both motivation and discipline and turns them into real-life action is having a plan for implementation. On his website of behavioral psychology, expert James Clear cites a hundred separate studies in a wide range of situations that reached the same conclusion: "People who explicitly state when and where their new behaviors are going to happen are much more likely to stick to their goals." Clear says that one reason this works is that, when our goals have defined times and spaces, our life's events and environments become the cues that remind us to follow through on our plans.

But just making these plans in our heads isn't enough. We need to write them down—and then we need to refer to them often. Otherwise, they'll simply disappear into the ether of our busy lives. *How* we write down our plan doesn't matter all that much, so long as we do it, in one way or another. As a rule, whatever is easiest for you to do is also the best way for you to do it.

Experiment a little until you find the method that's right for your needs and personality. Google Calendar is an option, if online planning works best. If you do use an online calendar of one sort or another, consider also writing your plan on paper, either before or after you put it online. Why? Because research indicates that when we write something with pen and paper (versus using a keyboard), the movement of our hands triggers a brain reaction that makes our words stick more easily in our memories.

The world is full of daily planners, but the best time-management planning system is the one you will actually use!

 INSPIRATION

Laura Vanderkam, author of *What the Most Successful People Do Before Breakfast,* emphasizes that no matter what time-management strategy you choose to use, the first hours of the day are the best time to get things accomplished. In a poll of twenty executives cited by Vanderkam, 90 percent said they wake up before 6 a.m. on weekdays.

PepsiCo CEO Indra Nooyi, for example, wakes at 4 a.m. and is in the office no later than 7 a.m.; Disney CEO Bob Iger gets up at 4:30 a.m. to read; Twitter and Square CEO Jack Dorsey is up at 5:30 a.m. to jog; former-Starbucks president (now at Kohl's) Michelle Gaas sets her alarm for 4:30 a.m. to go running; Gretchen Ruben, author of *The Happiness Project,* wakes up at 6 a.m. and works for an hour before her family rises. Before you start groaning, "But I'm just not a morning person," listen to some more of Vanderkam's advice.

First, she recommends that you start out slowly: Get up ten minutes earlier the first week, then fifteen minutes the next week, and twenty the week after that. Your body will adjust gradually and complain less. Work yourself up to a half an hour—and then see if you can take it higher than that. If you can't— if you find yourself tired during the day or getting discouraged—half an hour is still enough time for you to fit something important into your life. Personally, I recommend that you also make sure you're not robbing your sleep time at night by staying up doing things that don't contribute to your goals (like watching television or reading Facebook until after midnight).

Vanderkam also suggests that you use this extra time for the things you are most passionate about in life. That could be having more time to spend with your children or husband (which doesn't mean you get your kids up at 4:30 a.m. so you can play board games with them—but it might mean that you and they get up half an hour earlier so you can enjoy sitting down together to eat breakfast or read a chapter of a book together); it could be working on a special project that's hard to fit into your workday (like writing a novel or making a quilt); it could be meditating or praying (giving you more peace throughout the rest of your day); or it could be exercising (so that you have more energy through-out the rest of the day). Whatever it is, it should be something you genuinely enjoy and long to do. That way you'll look at that extra time in the morning as a gift you've given to yourself—rather than a sacrifice of precious sleep time.

#19

ALIGN REAL-LIFE TIME MANAGEMENT WITH YOUR GOALS

When life's demands vary from week to week, your goals can keep you on target.

The best laid plans of mice and men often go astray.

—ROBERT BURNS

Did you ever take ballet? There's a technique called "spotting" that dancers use when they're spinning around. Fixing their eyes on a specific spot helps them to maintain their balance and keeps them from feeling dizzy; it gives them greater control over their moves. When we're in crisis mode, we need to practice something similar. Our mission and goals become the "spot" we focus on.

Sometimes life turns into a whirling mass of confusion. It's inevitable, even in the most carefully planned lives. We can't control all of life's circumstances. So when that happens, we need to have a focus to hold us steady. That will only be possible if we have a time-management strategy that's flexible enough to still work under many different circumstances.

Say your daily plan depends on you getting up at 5:00 a.m. every morning and going to bed at 11:00 p.m. in order to fit in everything you've determined are priorities in your life—but then you get sick with the flu. Not only are you in bed for a week, but then afterward you also need more rest to get your strength back. The temptation will be to let everything slide. You'll say to yourself, "It's impossible right now to get anything accomplished that will get me closer to my goals. So I'm not going to even try. I'm going to forget all about those goals until life gets back to normal."

"Normal life," though, can be elusive. If we define "normal" as being those rare periods when we have absolute control over our lives, when everything goes according to schedule, then we'll find ourselves living our lives in constant crisis mode. Instead of having a plan that's flexible enough for all the big and small upsets that life brings, we'll be constantly stressed and overwhelmed. We'll never get very far toward achieving our goals, because our time-management system is too rigid to allow for real life. We built everything on doing things just one way—and then we get discouraged when that doesn't work.

Time-management strategies are only tools; they're not the end goals. If they don't help us reach our goals more easily, then they're not doing their jobs. This means that instead of focusing on our particular time-management systems, we need to focus on the end results we've chosen to work toward. When that's our focus, success no longer means forcing ourselves to stick to a tight schedule no matter what; success becomes moving a little closer toward those goals. When life falls apart, we can sit down and look at our values and priorities, and then figure out which parts of our plans aren't essential under the current circumstances. What things *can* we do that will inch us closer to the goals we've set for ourselves? And then we have to give ourselves the grace to do those things and not feel guilty about failing to follow a schedule that's impossible.

As much as I can, I keep my life organized. My routine is based on a daily time-management strategy, and our family life revolves around it. But when our house exploded, all of that totally went out the window. Fortunately, my overall personal mission statement and the big goals I'd sent for myself didn't go out the window too. They were what gave shape to the chaos my life had become. Working toward those goals looked different when we were moving from place to place trying to put a stable home back together for our family—but they still gave direction. They kept me focused.

Life can throw all kinds of challenges at us that will throw us off course if we let them. Two weeks after our second child was born, for example, I ran into a crisis I had no way of knowing would happen. My mom had come to help me out because my husband had to be away overseas on a business trip. As a self-employed mother, I was already back at work part-time, bringing the baby with me, while my mother stayed with our fifteen-month-old and helped us all adjust to our family's new reality. Then my mom's arm started swelling. After a day, it was twice its normal size; something clearly wasn't right. I left our older child, Jamisen, with a babysitter and loaded my mom and the newborn into the car to go to the emergency room. My mother ended up being admitted to the hospital with MRSA, a life-threatening, antibiotic-resistant infection.

I couldn't take our newborn baby, Lily, into the hospital, so I sat in the hospital parking lot until my brother could get there to sit with Lily in the car. And that's how we managed the next week. My brother and I would take turns holding Lily in the car, while the other one sat a shift with my mother. It wasn't easy. I hated being away from my baby, and I hated leaving little Jamisen. I was still working every day, and I had to be there because my chief operating officer was away.

Life was utterly crazy. Each morning, I would leave Jamisen with a babysitter, go to work with baby Lily, figure out when my brother could meet me at the hospital, go to the hospital, give my brother the baby, go see my mother, come back out of the hospital after washing my hands ten thousand times, retrieve the baby, go back to work, work a few hours—and then go back to the hospital and do all that again before I went home for the night. Then I'd go home and do mom stuff. As soon as I got the children to bed, I would do e-mail for work; I'd also wash dishes, do laundry, and defrost another meal so our household would keep running.

Through it all, I kept sight of my long-term goals, even though the short-term stuff had to be modified pretty radically. There were a few practical things that allowed me to maintain my sense of for-ward-looking direction, even in the midst of life being totally upside down. Aside from having a support network in the form of family and friends, I also had a freezer full of food I'd prepared before Lily's birth, which made my life that much easier during this unexpected crisis. I also used the Power of the Trudge (A Deeper Dive in Strategy #5), with a list of only three to five things that had to get done every day. Once those were done, I said to myself, "You did your three to five things that really matter, girlfriend, so go sit with your mom at the hospital for three hours. You're good."

There was no way I would have been able to come up with long-term goals in the midst of crisis. Luckily, I didn't have to because they were already in place. They gave me the framework I needed to give my day shape, even when everything was going crazy. They kept me focused and balanced until the day when my mother recovered, my COO was back at work, and my husband came home from his business trip.

When thrown into chaotic circumstances, adding even one extra responsibility to your day can make your life suddenly seem overwhelming. The temptation will be to let everything slide except the bare minimum of making an appearance at work and feeding your family. But take a moment to look at your life and see how you could adjust things—if only just a little bit—to help you keep on track.

Let's say that one of your goals is to do some form of aerobic exercise every day and feed your family a healthy home-cooked meal every evening. Then imagine that a close friend cracks her tooth and you have to rush her to the dentist. There goes your perfectly planned day! But, instead of reading magazines while in the dentist's waiting room, you choose to go outside and walk around the professional building or run up and down the stairs for a few minutes. Then, after returning your unfortunate friend to her home, you pick up some extra-nutritious takeout for your family. That would be one way you could fit in some aerobic exercise, even if for only fifteen minutes, and still provide your family with a healthy meal, even if it isn't homemade.

Or let's say one of your goals is to read more books on a particular topic and you have a huge deadline you're trying to meet at work. Instead of setting your reading aside while you're working so hard, could you listen to books on tape during your morning commute?

These are just a couple of examples. If you can't imagine either one working for you, don't set aside the entire principle! Each set of circumstances will be different, and the solutions you discover will be uniquely your own—but you'll find them if you look for them.

And don't forget to use the calmer, more predictable times of your life to prep for the inevitable big and small crises that life always brings. That might mean making double portions of each meal and freezing half for those nights when you won't have time to cook, or it might be finding a good prep-and-cook delivery service to fall back on when you need extra help with meals. It could entail stocking up on books-on-tape so you have some on hand the next time you need them—because if you're feeling frantic and overwhelmed by work, the last thing you probably want to do is spend time at a bookstore looking for taped reading material or scrolling through Audible.com to find the best book to download to your device. Whatever you do, it will involve anticipating things that will help you get more smoothly through the unpredictable periods of your life and *still* live your Best Days Ever!

 BUSINESS APPLICATION

Naturally, just as individual lives can be upset by a crisis, so can businesses. Do you have a disaster preparedness plan for your business? If you don't, you're in good company. According to *Inc.* magazine, half of all businesses do not have a disaster recovery plan. It's not just hotels that need maps for where to go in case of emergency; businesses need them in a figurative way. According to federal data, 43 percent of businesses that close following a natural disaster don't reopen, and 29 percent close two years later.

The Small Business Administration recommends creating a preparedness program (sometimes called a business continuity plan or disaster recovery plan) for your business that includes identifying critical business systems, creating an emergency communications plan, and testing business systems.

The form crises take depends in part on what type of business you're in, but these are some of the most common:

Natural disasters: It doesn't have to be a hurricane or major earthquake for your business to be thrown off course. Flooding caused by burst water pipes or heavy rain can be nearly as destructive.

Theft or vandalism: Losing computer equipment or other machinery essential to your business can be devastating to your operations.

Power cuts: Loss of power can have serious consequences, when almost all businesses now depend on IT for their daily function. Many businesses have other machinery and processes that depend on electricity.

IT system failure: Computer viruses, Denial of Service attacks, or other system failures will affect you and your employees' ability to work effectively.

Loss or illness of key staff: If any of your staff is central to the running of your business, consider how you would cope if they were suddenly not there. Are there any processes or skills that depend solely on certain individuals? Now is your opportunity to write Standards of Work for those key positions outlining tasks and responsibilities.

Crises affecting your business reputation: How would you cope, for example, in the event of a product recall? Who would you call? What would your communication strategy be?

 MAKE IT PERSONAL

None of us can predict all the big crises in life (like a car accident—or your house exploding). But there are some crises that reoccur in life that we *can* anticipate. For example, unless our health is consistently perfect, we can probably predict that we'll get a cold or even the flu this year. If we have children, odds are good that they'll get sick more than once during the year. If our work is the sort that has tight deadlines, it is probably safe to say we'll find ourselves scrambling to meet them at some point.

- So take an honest look at your life—and then list at least three things that are likely to happen in the next few months that you could throw off your schedule. Anticipate some of those life wrenches: family illness, big promotion, relationship troubles, etc.

- Now describe how each of those circumstances has the potential to upset your priorities. Which of your goals will each circumstance hinder?

- What are alternative ways for you to still meet your goals, even when these circumstances occur? Think outside the box. Having a fallback plan in place before the crisis occurs is a better strategy than trying to come up with one when you're already stressed out and overwhelmed. List your fallback plans and keep them handy.

- Are there things you can do *now*—today, tomorrow, this week—to help you prep for these events?

 INSPIRATION

Life coach and behavioral psychology expert James Clear recommends using the "if-then" strategy to cope with the unexpected situations that arise in all our lives. "You simply plan for unexpected situations," he says on his website, by using this phrase:

If _____ happens, then I'll _____.

Here are a few examples of how that might work:

If my meeting runs over and I don't have time to work out this afternoon, then I'll wake up early tomorrow and run.

If my husband has to handle the bedtime routine while I work late this week, then I'll spend Saturday with the kids doing something fun and interesting.

If my mother calls in the evening when I normally meditate, then I won't turn on the TV until after I've meditated.

If I must stay home from work because my child is sick, then I will spend at least an hour working on my laptop toward one of my work goals.

These aren't excuses, Clear emphasizes, nor are they ways to rationalize procrastinating things we really need to do (and could do). Instead, he says, "The 'if–then' strategy gives you a clear plan for overcoming the unexpected stuff, which means it's less likely that you'll be swept away by the urgencies of life. You can't control when little emergencies happen to you, but you don't have to be a victim of them either."

#20

KEEP A BALANCE BETWEEN YOUR WORK LIFE, YOUR FAMILY LIFE, AND YOUR PERSONAL LIFE

Nurturing your own identity will make you stronger in other areas of your life.

"In art and dream you may proceed with abandon. In life you may proceed with balance and stealth."

—PATTI SMITH

We talk about the empty-nest syndrome—that moment when parents realize that the center of their attention for the past eighteen years has moved on to a new phase of life, leaving them behind—but few of us consider that our work life can have as strong an effect on our lives, if we let it, as our children do. Losing our work, for whatever reason, can be just as painful as the time when our children leave home. Neither experience has to shake us to the core of our identities if we've kept our lives balanced.

The level of devastation parents experience when they enter the empty-nest phase of their lives depends on whether they had tended to their own lives all along. If they haven't—if they've neglected hobbies and friends and their own relationships with each other, while focusing only on their offspring's sports, musical activities, grades, and social lives—then they'll have an aching, gaping hole at the center of their lives that will take time to fill. They will have to figure out their own identities all over again. They'll be asking themselves: "What am I going to do with all this extra time? Do I even like my partner anymore? Do I have friends anymore? Oh my gosh! What were my hobbies? Who *am* I if I'm not primarily a parent?" On the other hand, if the parents have all along maintained strong personal lives of their own, then they'll still miss the kids of course, but they'll have a central core that remains unshaken.

The same sort of thing also applies to our business lives. Nurturing the life we lead outside of our professions will help us maintain our balance, no matter what happens at work. My personal goals and my business goals do not overlap. For me to have a joy-filled life—my Best-Day-Ever life—I need to have personal habits, personal hobbies, and personal dreams and aspirations that are outside my business. Otherwise, I'll constantly take my work home with me. It's easy to lack boundaries between my home life and my professional life. While my kids are asking me questions and my husband is telling me about his day, I'll be thinking about how to redo my website or figuring out how we can ship more boxes per day. I'll miss out on the precious present moment with the people I love most.

Business ebbs and flows. Sometimes things go well; sometimes not so well. Sometimes, everything can totally fall apart. Having personal goals that give us an ongoing plan outside our work will keep us steady though the ups and downs of the business world. No matter how much we love our work, without a robust personal life, we will eventually find ourselves burned out and stressed professionally—and that tension will spill over into the other areas of our lives as well.

Meanwhile, because we love our families so much, it's equally easy to focus too much of our identities in that area of our lives. Young children demand so much of our attention that it can be hard to tell where they begin and we leave off. Especially if we've made the choice to stay at home while our kids are young, we can feel totally absorbed by their needs. When our kids are older, we face other challenges. Teenagers don't need the constant care and attention that a baby does—but they can be equally demanding in different ways.

Losing the boundaries in our lives happens surprisingly easily. We must be intentional about maintaining them; we must consciously set goals for ourselves that will keep us focused on the things that are important for us as individuals, not just as professionals or as parents. While we're protecting our inner balance, that strong sense of who we are no matter what happens in our other worlds, we will also be helping ourselves become better professionals and better parents. How you are personally is how you are professionally—and how you are personally is also how you will be as a parent. If you generate energy and joy in your personal life, then that will carry over into both your parenting and your work.

Keeping our lives balanced isn't easy. And because we're human beings, perfection—maintaining the ideal balance—is impossible!

We'll never be able to set permanent boundaries between work, family, and our individual needs, and then expect they'll remain fixed and rigid for all time. Instead, I like to think of these boundary lines as semi-permeable membranes, flexible enough to adapt to the needs of whatever is going on in my life.

It's inevitable that life at times will spin us around and knock us down. When that happens, go back and reread Strategy #11 (Find Your "Why"), realign again with your circumstances, find a new balance, and keep your focus on living your Best Day Ever.

 BUSINESS APPLICATION

Neil Grimmer, co-founder and CEO of Plum Organics, has this to say about the relationship between your work life and "the rest of your life": "Whether you're an entrepreneur starting a company or you're working for someone else, work should be an extension of your life. If that's not the case, if you don't feel like work is an extension of who you are, you always will have a trade-off between work and life. We have a saying: 'BYOS.' It stands for 'Bring Your Own Self.' And it means that there should never be a separation between who our employees are outside these offices and who they are inside. Really, it's all about passion. Every one of us has the opportunity to lead a passion-driven life; we just need to put the time in to understand what we expect from ourselves."

MAKE IT PERSONAL

- Take some time to think about your life. What are the most important areas of your life? (These could be parenting, being a professional, being a spouse, being the caregiver for needy elderly parents, or anything else that takes up significant space in both your time and your heart.) List them.

- Now ask yourself: Do I also have a strong sense of my own identity at the same time that I'm functioning in these various roles? If not, which roles have begun to take over my sense of who I am?

- What are three things you can do this week to nurture your own identity? These needn't take a lot of time. Even small things can give us the stable internal core we need.

INSPIRATION

This folktale—which I've modernized a bit—is an excellent reminder about finding balance in life:

A businesswoman had to travel to a poor nation because her company was thinking about building a factory there. Her hotel was on the beach, and one morning, as she sat drinking her coffee and watching the tide, she saw a fisherman unloading his catch onto a nearby dock.

"Wow!" she said. "You certainly caught a lot of fish. How long did that take you?"

"Not long," the fisherman said.

"You mean if you had stayed out longer, you could have caught even more?" the woman asked.

"Yes," the man answered.

"Then why didn't you stay out longer?" asked the woman.

"Because this is enough for me and my family," explained the fisherman.

"So what do you do with the rest of your time?"

"I play with my children, I spend time with my wife, I take a nap. Then in the evening, I go into the village to visit my friends. We sing a few songs together. I go home happy."

The woman shook her head. "You'll never get ahead like that."

"Ahead of what?" the man asked.

"I mean you'll never get rich if you don't work harder. Let me give you some advice. You should spend more time on the water fishing. Then you can sell the extra fish, make more money, and buy a bigger boat."

"And after that?"

"With the bigger boat, you can catch more fish and make more money. Then you can buy two or three boats and later hire more people to operate a fleet of fishing trawlers. Eventually, instead of selling your fish here on the docks to a middleman, you can start to negotiate directly with the processing plants. After a while you would be able to open your own plant. Then you could leave this little village and move to a big city. From there you could operate the whole enterprise."

"How long would that take?" asked the fisherman.

The woman thought a moment. "Probably about twenty years. But maybe less if you work really hard."

"And after that?"

"Well, that's when it gets really exciting," the woman said. "When the business gets really big, you can sell stock in the company and make millions!"

"Wow, millions! What happens after that?" asked the fisherman.

The woman smiled. "After that you'll be able to retire on the coast, do some fishing, play with your grandchildren, spend time with your wife, and take naps whenever you want. In the evenings you will be able to go out singing with your friends. Doesn't that sound great?"

The fisherman looked puzzled. "But I do all that now. Why would I leave the life I love for so many years, just to have again what I already have now?" He shook his head and walked away.

#21

PROFITABILITY EQUALS OPPORTUNITY

Think of money as a power tool.

A wise person should have money in their head,
but not in their heart.

—JONATHAN SWIFT

When I started Bramble Berry, I had no real business experience (except for my hamster-breeding business). I didn't have any money yet, either, but what I did have was enthusiasm. When orders started to come in, I was so excited that I was willing to take calls at five in the morning from people who were on East Coast time. I used my dad's credit card processing machine to process the orders, and I packed orders on a desk I had made from an old door supported on old fragrance container drums as the legs. It was not a sophisticated operation—but I was so thrilled I didn't care.

I didn't start Bramble Berry with the goal of getting rich. Since money wasn't my primary value, I didn't focus a whole lot on finances. I did do a basic profit-and-loss every month—here's what I sold the product for; here's what the product cost me; here's what it cost me to pay my telephone; and so on—and things looked fine to me. On paper, it always looked as though there was money on that bottom line. So I would buy more inventory; then I'd add a few more items to my catalog; and every month, there was always money on the bottom line of my profit-and-loss. I did this for years, always thinking things were going fine.

One thing I could never understand, though, was why there was never any money to pay myself. Despite the positive numerals on the bottom line, there was never any actual money left in the bank account. In fact, I was putting more and more money on credit cards. I couldn't understand what was happening.

Of course, profits do not equal cash flow. Growth sucks cash. One of the reasons I didn't figure this out quickly enough, though, was because my first mission statement as a company went something like this: "The love of the craft will always drive everything I do. Profit will never be a goal for the company." Well, when you have stated that your goal is to not make money, guess what? You don't make money.

And that's how I found myself $247,000 in debt at a very young age, all on credit cards. People can't imagine now being able to get that far in debt. That wouldn't happen in today's financial world. However, it was definitely something that you could do back in the late 2000s before the crash. Credit card offers kept coming in the mail—and I kept using them to keep my business afloat.

Finally, I had to stop and look at what I was doing. I knew I needed to change things, so I spent some time digging down deep to figure out how I could meld the need to actually make money (because that's why companies exist) with the love and gratitude I felt for my job. Because that's what it came down to: I felt guilty for being paid money for something I loved.

I worked hard, using Verne Harnish's book, *Mastering the Rockefeller Habits*, to think about my business priorities, based on accurate data that had a well-organized rhythm to maintain alignment with my priorities and to drive accountability. I needed to determine the values that would guide my company to long-term, stable profitability.

Then I hired a business coach who helped me come up with a two-year plan to pay off my credit card debt. That two-year plan was basically all work and no play. I didn't take a paycheck. I didn't give any raises. I didn't add many new products to our line. Instead, I had to be super creative about the new products I was adding and how I was adding them. I needed to come up with new ways to present what I was already carrying to keep people interested and still make me look new and fresh. My entire focus was on chipping down that debt.

I also articulated new values for my company's mission statement. One of them was *profitability equals opportunity*. Profitability means I am able to pay my staff a fair wage. Profitability means I am able to donate to worthy nonprofits. Profitability means I am able to have savings so that if something ever went wrong, I could keep paying my staff. Profitability means I can take care of myself and my family, so that my business is sustainable.

Back in Strategy #2, I said that your passion is something you have to offer the world that it needs—and that's true. But while money can never be the sole reason you follow your passion, it does have to play a role. Don't assume that being passionate about something means you shouldn't also be financially responsible about it.

Your "why" needs to live side-by-side with finances. Unless you have unlimited private funds or a wealthy donor who is willing to support you, think carefully about how your passion connects with your financial resources. Whether you want to start a business or fund a passion for helping others in your community, smart financial planning is essential.

If you're like I was when I first went into business, and you feel uncomfortable focusing on money, think of it as an essential tool you need to make things happen. You wouldn't try to build a house without a saw—or sew a quilt without a needle—or bake a batch of cookies without an oven. Without each of these necessary tools, you wouldn't have a house, a quilt, or a batch of cookies; all you'd have are dreams. In a similar way, money is the power tool you need to make your passion practical. It's what brings your vision into the real world. Your profitability means you increase opportunities for yourself and everyone around you.

Smart financial management gives us peace of mind. We can go to sleep without anxiety about where the next dollar is coming from; we can relax and enjoy our passion, without always worrying if there will be enough money in the bank to cover overhead. Money isn't the *reason* why we pursue our passions—but it *is* a tool that helps us build our Best Day Ever.

 BUSINESS APPLICATION

Annual goal-setting must be integrated with creating an annual budget both at work and at home. At my business, we ask ourselves: "Given our goals for the year, what kinds of financial things do we need to support it?" Then, once a month, we sit down with both our goals and the budget. We look at where we're out of alignment and where we are in alignment. If any of our goals are off track, we go back to the budget and ask: "Did we spend enough money on it? Did we put enough time into it? Do we need to allocate more of both? If there's not enough money to allocate more toward that goal, let's figure it out." We make the practical decisions that need to be made. This yearly and monthly rhythm makes sure that we never get too far out of alignment.

 MAKE IT PERSONAL

- Take some time to think about your attitude toward money and finances. Now, try to summarize your thoughts into a single sentence. Here are some possible examples:

  □ Money is the root of all evil.

  □ I'm not the kind of person to make a lot of money.

  □ Money is scarce—there's only so much to go around.

  □ It would be greedy and selfish for me to focus on making money.

  □ Not having enough money scares me.

  □ Money scares me.

  □ I feel ashamed when I think about money because I know I've made some foolish financial decisions.

- □ I hate money so much that I don't like to even think about it.
- □ I love money because I feel more in control of my life when I have it.
- □ It's just money—so I don't care whether I lose it.
- □ I worry about financial stability all the time, even when my bank account looks good.
- □ I'm never sure who I can trust when it comes to making financial decisions.

- Now ask yourself: How does my attitude about money shape my financial situation right now? Remember that how we think about things is the reality we usually live. Describe how your money attitude is currently either empowering your life or holding you back.

- Is your money attitude getting in the way of living your Best Day Ever? If so, how could you change your attitude to form a solid financial foundation for your life? Write a new money statement—and then reread it often. Here are a few examples:

  - □ Money is a tool I can use to make the world a better place.
  - □ Money gives me opportunities.
  - □ Having money makes me happy because it gives me more options.
  - □ I have the ability to learn more about smart money management so I can feel confident in the decisions I make.

▫ I always have a back-up plan or two so I can successfully ride out the ups and downs of my financial health.

 INSPIRATION

If money management isn't something you enjoy, Laura D. Adams, author of *Money Girl's Smart Moves to Deal with Your Debt*, suggests that you use her strategy:

"I look at managing my money as if it were a part-time job. The time you spend monitoring your finances will pay off. You can make real money by cutting expenses and earning more interest on savings and investments. I'd challenge you to find a part-time job where you could potentially earn as much money for just an hour or two of your time."

Adams stresses that the first step to using money wisely to empower your life is to monitor inflow and outflow, so that you are in touch with your financial reality.

#22

HEALTH IS NOT A MATTER OF LUCK

Taking care of your body allows you to live your best life.

Take care of your body.

It's the only place you have to live.

—JIM ROHN

Sometimes I hear people say things like, "I have the worst luck when it comes to getting sick. Seems like I catch everything that's going around." Or, they'll cross their fingers and say, "I sure hope I can get through the winter without getting sick so much this year." We act as though we have no control over our own health. But actually, we do.

As busy as our lives are, it's easy to put our own health last. After rushing around all day, taking care of a million different things in a zillion separate directions, all we want to do is eat some junk food, have a drink, and watch some mindless TV. It seems harmless enough.

It's not. We hurt ourselves when we neglect our bodies. We don't give our bodies what they need to function at top capacity. As a result, every area of our lives suffers.

Needless to say, if you are rundown and sick with a cold, then you're probably not going to have your Best Day Ever. It's hard to choose to be happy when you're exhausted. We forget that our brain is a body part, just as much as our stomach and lungs. Simply put, our brain doesn't work as well when we've deprived it of the many things it needs to keep up with the many functions it performs. We're less efficient and not as creative; we don't think as clearly; and we're more prone to emotional upsets.

I'm not saying that if we eat right, exercise, and get the sleep we need, we'll *never* get sick. If we make a plan to meet our bodies' needs, though—and carry through on it—we will be healthier. With better nutrition, regular exercise, and more sleep, our immune systems grow stronger. We're better able to cope with stress at home and at work.

This information about health is nothing new—most of us already know the basics of a healthy lifestyle. Yet knowing doesn't equal action.

Action comes in different forms, but it always starts with a plan to make it happen. When you make your yearly, weekly, and daily plans, include your body's needs too. Schedule exercise. Plan your meals. Make your eating decisions—groceries, snacks, work lunches, and dinner engagements—ahead of time, when you're not hungry. Commit to a certain number of hours of sleep per night. In addition to the framework of a plan, be thoughtful about the tiny, everyday choices you make.

For example, who hasn't wanted to stay up past a normal bedtime to read a magazine or finish a book? I know I'm guilty! Going to bed on time to get seven (or more) hours of sleep so that the next day goes better is a seemingly insignificant choice that ends up making a big difference in the end.

On her website, Dr. Christine Northrop recommends that we think of ourselves as our "own best mothers." As parents, we usually work hard to make sure our children are as healthy as possible. We monitor snacks, pack lunches, make healthy dinners; we send our kids off to bed at a regular time most nights; and we give them opportunities to run around and play. Then we fail to give ourselves the same nurturing care. However, if we take Northrop's advice to "treat yourself like an ideal mother would," we will think of ourselves as an equally important member of the family, someone who deserves our utmost care and commitment.

Feeling strong and happy is powerful motivation for continuing to say yes to healthy habits. The foundation for a Best-Day-Ever lifestyle is adequate sleep, low to no alcohol, no sugar, appropriate hydration, essential fatty acids and vitamin D intake, nutrient-dense "ancient" grains (ditching processed gluten grains), and getting twenty minutes of intentional movement daily. Taken individually, all of these things seem doable—and they are. Together, they form a powerful system that's the baseline for more energy, health, vitality, and longevity.

BUSINESS APPLICATION

Getting enough sleep is a performance-enhancement tool in the business world. While it's true that different bodies have different needs, it's also true that adults need a minimum number of hours of sleep per night. The National Sleep Foundation sets that number as seven. Of course, there are many factors that can make this number go up and down (like pregnancy, sleep deprivation/interruption, or overall health). But for our purposes, we're going to use seven hours of sleep as a baseline. When we get at least that much sleep, we feel better, we're more productive at work, more energetic, less foggy, and more focused on what's most important to us. We're even better at learning new things and being creative!

Our bodies use sleep time to rejuvenate and heal. Ever wonder why you're so tired when you get sick? It's because your body is trying to force you to go to sleep so it can work on making you better. While we're drooling on our pillows, our bodies are hard at work healing heart and blood vessels, releasing hormones that boost muscle mass, and repairing cells and tissues. The two hormones that control appetite (ghrelin and leptin) are also main-tained by sleep.

Sleep also provides a multitude of mental benefits. While our bodies are healing, our brains aren't sleeping on the job; they're using that time to form new pathways that give us the ability to learn new information and help us remember. To help you get enough quality sleep, here are some practical tips:

- Don't work from your bedroom.

- Try to go to bed at about the same time every night.

- Turn your phone to silent when you go to bed; getting text messages in the middle of the night will affect the quality of rest your body is getting.

- Finally, make sure you sleep at least seven hours a night.

By getting enough sleep, you will have more consistent energy levels, enjoy better productivity at work, and your mind will be more focused. Now that's a no-brainer!

 MAKE IT PERSONAL

- Over the next week, keep a record of how much sleep you get, what you eat, and how long you move your body each day. Then make a note of how you felt during the day, using a scale of 1 to 10 for energy level, mental focus, and mood. At the end of the week, look at this record. If you're seeing a lot of numbers that are 5 or less in the energy, focus, and mood columns, you may not be taking adequate care of your body. Pay attention to what affects you negatively: Too much sugar instead of complex carbohydrates? Skipping meals? Not enough sleep?

	HRS. OF SLEEP	FOOD	MINS. OF EXERCISE	ENERGY	FOCUS	MOOD
DAY 1						
DAY 2						
DAY 3						
DAY 4						
DAY 5						
DAY 6						
DAY 7						

- If you have not been caring for your body adequately, what can you do differently this week? Make a specific plan and write it down.

 INSPIRATION

In his book *Integrative Nutrition: Feed Your Hunger for Health and Happiness*, author Joshua Rosenthal says:

We can, and must, develop dialogue and relatedness with our body because it's talking to us all the time. And please remember, your body loves you. It does everything it can to keep you alive and functioning. You can feed it garbage, and it will take it and digest it for you. You can deprive it of sleep, but still it gets you up and running next morning. You can drink too much alcohol, and it will eliminate it from your system. It loves you unconditionally and does its best to allow you to live the life you came here for. The real issue in this relationship is not whether your body loves you, but whether you love your body. In any relationship, if one partner is loving, faithful, and supportive, it's easy for the other to take that person for granted. That's what most of us do with our bodies. It is time for you to shift this, and working to understand your cravings is one of the best places to begin. Then you can build a mutually loving relationship with your own body.

Working hard isn't the same as peak performance.

Sleep is that golden chain that ties health and our bodies together.

—THOMAS DEKKER

As busy workers, family members, and community participants, we often feel as though we don't have enough time in the day. But now, as we dive deeper into the importance of rest and renewal, we recognize that when we don't think we have enough time in our lives to do everything, sleep is often the first thing that suffers. We act as though sleep is expendable. Some of us even seem to pride ourselves on how few hours of sleep we get because of our busy days, as though lack of sleep proves what dedicated and efficient people we are. Of course, as discussed previously, it indicates just the opposite. Lack of sleep can make us inefficient and less productive.

Ongoing sleep deficiency has been linked to an increased risk of chronic and serious diseases—such as heart disease, kidney disease, high blood pressure, diabetes, and stroke—while adequate sleep has been shown to strengthen our immune system, organ health, and vital physical, mental, and emotional processes.

Lack of sleep can even make us more likely to gain weight. Have you ever noticed that when you're tired, you want to eat more? This is partly because sleep helps maintain a healthy balance of the hormones that tell us whether we are hungry or full. When we don't get enough sleep, the hunger hormone levels go up, while the fullness hormones go down. Sleep deficiency also results in higher than normal blood-sugar levels, which may increase our risk for diabetes.

Our society praises and rewards people who work hard—but hard work isn't the same as peak performance. People who are sleep deficient are less productive in every area of their lives. They take longer to finish tasks, have a slower reaction time, and make more mistakes. A 2016 finding from the AAA Foundation for Traffic Safety indicates that drivers who have had too little sleep are no different from those who have had three or four drinks and are too drunk to drive.

The evidence is overwhelming: With adequate sleep, you'll get more done in fewer hours—and you'll feel happier and healthier while doing it!

SIDE EFFECTS FROM MISSING SLEEP

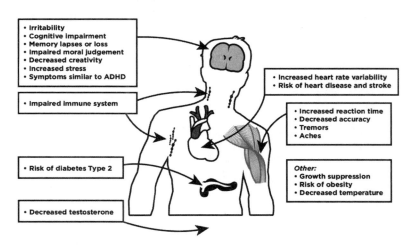

- Irritability
- Cognitive impairment
- Memory lapses or loss
- Impaired moral judgement
- Decreased creativity
- Increased stress
- Symptoms similar to ADHD

- Impaired immune system

- Risk of diabetes Type 2

- Decreased testosterone

- Increased heart rate variability
- Risk of heart disease and stroke

- Increased reaction time
- Decreased accuracy
- Tremors
- Aches

Other:
- Growth suppression
- Risk of obesity
- Decreased temperature

MAKE IT PERSONAL

Take some time to honestly consider your sleep habits. What areas could you improve? Are you falling short of adequate rest? What hinders you from managing your sleep better? Look at the earlier data you collected to build from. (If you like high-tech solutions, the app Sleep Cycle can be a great help. I use this app in airplane mode every night.)

Here's something to keep in mind: If you're like me, you may love to scroll through Twitter and read the *New York Times* as a way to wind down and relax before settling down to sleep—but studies are very clear that the blue light emitted from our smartphones and tablets impedes quality of sleep and adversely affects circadian rhythm. This is an area I need to improve. What are *your* areas?

The National Sleep Foundation offers these tips for improving the quality of your sleep:

- **Stick to a sleep schedule.** Try to go to bed and wake up at the same time, even on the weekends. This helps to regulate your body's clock, which can help you fall asleep and stay asleep for the night.

- **Practice a relaxing bedtime ritual.** A relaxing, routine activity right before bedtime helps separate your sleep time from activities that can cause excitement, stress, or anxiety, which can make it more difficult to fall asleep, get sound and deep sleep, or remain asleep. A relaxing ritual could be meditation or prayer, reading a book, or listening to music. Watching television is *not* a good bedtime ritual!

- **Avoid naps in the afternoon.** "Power napping" may help you get through the day, but if you find that you can't fall asleep at bedtime, eliminating even short catnaps may help.

- **Exercise daily.** Vigorous exercise is best, but even light exercise can help you sleep better at night.

- **Taper off caffeine intake throughout the day.** Caffeine after 3 p.m. will affect your sleep because caffeine stays in the body up to six hours. Aim to taper off any coffee consumption after noon, and cut out all caffeine drinks (green tea, black tea, white tea, yerba mate, etc.) by 3 p.m. at the latest.

- **Evaluate your room.** Design your sleep environment to establish the conditions you need for rest and renewal. Have comfortable pillows, and make the room attractive, peaceful, and inviting. Blue light (smartphones, iPads, etc.) should be turned off at least an hour before bed (ideally, three hours before bed, but that isn't realistic for many of us). Your bedroom should be free from any light, should be cool (between 60 and 67 degrees), and should be free from any noise that can disturb your sleep. If you can't control all of these factors, consider using blackout curtains, eye shades, ear plugs, "white noise" machines, humidifiers, fans, and other devices. Make sure your mattress is comfortable and supportive. The life expectancy for most good quality mattresses is about nine or ten years, so if you have an older mattress, it may no longer be doing its job well.

Pick one of these tips—and plan to make one change this week to improve the quality of your sleep. When I evaluated my own sleep needs, I ended up investing in not only a new mattress but also in a new fancy pillow and sheets. After all, we spend as much time in bed as we do at the office. We should make it as comfortable and healthy as possible. Write down your plan for improving your sleep habits.

Come back to this exercise in a month to reassess. How well have you followed through on your plan? What worked well? What made it hard to follow? If you saw improvement, note any differences this made in the way you felt physically and emotionally. If not, consider taking further action to adjust your life so that your daily routine supports healthy sleep habits.

For more information on this topic, I recommend *Sleep Smarter: 21 Essential Strategies to Sleep Your Way to a Better Body, Better Health, and Bigger Success* by Shawn Stevenson.

#23

FUEL YOUR BODY

A healthy diet supports your optimal life.

Let food be thy medicine and medicine be thy food.

—HIPPOCRATES

If I could go back and give some strong advice to my twenty-year-old self, here's what I would include (among many other things!) in my self-lecture: "Change the way you eat! Fuel your body for the life you want to lead in the future. Having energy that is consistent and reliable is a result of a well-fueled body. Good nutrition is what will make you able to bounce out of bed happily every morning. You can't work toward goals if you're too tired to get out of bed or if your body is aching because of the extra weight you're putting on your joints. Immerse yourself in the nutrition information coming out of the slow-food and vegan movements. Educate yourself—and then take that knowledge and act on it."

Remember in Strategy #2 when we talked about your unique experience mixing with your personal passion bringing something the world needs? This is another example of that. Growing up in a mostly vegetarian household with strict dietary rules (which as a kid I often complained about!) combined with an early passion of mine—cooking—to create the perfect opportunity to learn about the benefits of good nutrition. I was exposed every day to healthy cooking, and I had fun being creative in the kitchen while helping my mother prepare meals for our family.

Today, I still love cooking. In fact, I'm obsessed with healthy cooking and nutrition to the point that I went back to school to get my nutritional therapy certification.

My current passion and drive has its roots not only in my upbringing, with its focus on a healthy diet, but also in my father's profession as a doctor. When I was younger, I worked summers in my dad's clinic. All I did was filing and scheduling for his partner, but in those pre-HIPAA days, I was exposed to the effects of chronic illness as I listened to the nurses and doctors discuss their cases. I saw what poor diet and a lack of movement could do to the human body. The impact of those experiences is part of who I am today. I run fitness and health challenges, because I know the difference that diet and exercise can make to your energy levels and longevity.

The way I eat today has been shaped by those experiences and also books like *The Calorie Myth* (Jonathan Bailor), *Crazy Sexy Diet* (Kris Carr), *Bulletproof Diet* (Dave Asprey), and Michael Pollen's brilliant synopsis of healthy eating in *The Omnivore's Dilemma* (eat mostly plants and not too much).

Here is the basic blueprint I follow for optimum nutrition:

- ***Limited alcohol***: Yes, this is a tough one for some of us! But alcohol slows down our metabolism and disrupts our sleep, making us foggy the next day. You may not even know you're in a fog because that fog has become your "normal."

- *Limited dairy*: I know, cheese tastes delicious. If I were marooned on a desert island, I would probably be fine if I had an endless supply of cheese and sourdough bread. Our bodies do not love cheese, though, or most dairy for that matter. So, your Best Day Ever probably doesn't include a lot of cheese or milk or cream. Instead, it can include kefir and some Greek yogurts.

- *Veggies at every meal:* If you focus on the veggies first, the rest of the food falls in line. Aim to get 50 percent veggies at every meal and then fill in the protein and fats after that. Some delicious grass-fed butter (Kerrygold) on most veggies makes them taste amazing, as do olive oil, salt/pepper, and lemon juice.

- *Healthy fats:* Healthy fats often come in the form of a supplement, such as fish oil, evening primrose oil, or Barleans Total Omega. Our brains run on fats, so unless you're eating fish daily, you're probably not getting enough. Get a supplement and start moisturizing your skin from the inside out while also helping your mood swings and brain functioning.

- *No Sugar:* No sugar at all. Ever. Sorry. I know you love it. I love it too. That's why it's more addicting than cocaine. Cut out honey too. I want it. You want it. And it just keeps our bodies dependent on sugar and craving sweets. Remember, life is a marathon, not a sprint. This means we need long-lasting energy for the entire day, not a quick sugar rush that will get us revved up for only the next hour.

- **Supplements:** Generally, I'm a fan of getting all our nutrients from food, but in some cases, this isn't possible. Some nutrients that we are often low in are Vitamin D (unless you live in Hawaii or California or Arizona), iron, and B vitamins. You can confirm all of your levels with a test you order yourself at Wellness FX or ask your doctor to order them (insurance will sometimes pay for these tests).

- **Wheat is not your friend:** The reason wheat is not your friend doesn't have so much to do with the actual wheat (though the wheat we eat now is not the wheat our grandparents ate!) as much as what the wheat is usually in: pasta, doughnuts, bread, and sweets. If you're going to eat gluten, stick to the ancient grains like farro, amaranth, quinoa, and others. They often have amino acids our bodies crave and some building blocks for protein.

- **Hydration:** Drink half of your body weight in ounces of water each day. Our bodies depend on water to survive, and our cells and organs also need water in order to function properly. Keep a water bottle with you during the day. Is regular water too boring for your taste buds? Try adding a slice of lemon, lime, or grapefruit, or drinking herbal tea.

I believe these are the best nutrition rules to follow—but you don't need to eat exactly like I do. Find a healthy way of eating that's right for you. Whether you eat meat or you're vegetarian or vegan, if you follow a paleo diet or you're a pescatarian, practice the really big things: drink enough water, cut out as much sugar as you possibly can from your diet, and make sure you're not eating too many refined carbohydrates. Those are the major things that help you have the energy to run your busy work life, your full family life, and all the other jam-packed parts of your days.

Remember, your physical energy is one of your greatest natural resources. Protect it by systematizing your nutrition and hydration through small, daily habits that will become easier by the day (see Strategy #4). And don't forget the real reason why nutrition is an essential part of the Best-Day-Ever life: Without it, you won't have the physical and emotional strength needed to live out your mission.

BUSINESS APPLICATION

"Food is like a pharmaceutical compound that affects the brain," reports Fernando Gómez-Pinilla, a UCLA professor of neurosurgery and physiological science who has researched the effects of nutrition on our ability to engage in mental work. This has direct and practical implications for the business world. According to research collected by the World Health Organization (WHO), daily healthy nutrition increases work productivity by as much as 20 percent, and a study from the Health Enhancement Research Organization found that employees who ate healthily all day long increased productivity by 25 percent.

It's not just productivity that suffers when you're not eating nutrient-dense foods. It's also attendance at work. It's estimated that each year, employee absences cost employers between $2,650 and $3,600 per year per employee. One of the ways to help encourage your team to stay healthy is through formal workplace health programs or by providing healthy food options. A few years ago, we noticed that our younger, college-age workforce was falling sick more often than we could sustain in our busy season. We also noticed that they seemed to eat an unusually large amount of quick grab'n'go snacks such as Pop Tarts and Red Bull for breakfast. We started providing healthy meals twice a week, flu shot clinics, started multiple sports teams, and hired a professional towel service to wash shop towels so they weren't breeding grounds for germs. The combination of all these things helped to reduce our employee absenteeism.

MAKE IT PERSONAL

Are you fueling your body properly? A good way to find out is to use one of the online food trackers or a daily nutrition app. If you do an online search, you'll discover a long list of these. Find one that is both easy and convenient to use and that also compares your daily intake with your daily nutritional requirements. Or you could keep a food journal and write down every single thing you eat for one week.

- After you've tracked your food intake for a week, summarize the results. Where is your nutrition adequate? In what ways is it falling short?

- Now make a plan to do at least one thing differently in the week to come. It might be eating a healthy breakfast, it might be packing a healthy lunch to bring to work, or it could be deciding to say no to all junk food. Pick just one thing that you can commit to doing and write it down.

Consider keeping an ongoing food journal. Research has found that people who keep a food journal of one sort or another are twice as likely to stick to a dietary plan.

Additionally, accountability groups are another solid way to stay on track with whatever healthy eating plan you've committed to. One of the reasons that Weight Watchers is the most successful weight loss plan when it comes to keeping weight off long term is the support and accountability that happens at weekly weigh-ins and/or their online community. You can form your own accountability group of like-minded individuals looking to improve their health through nutrition. Share your food logs daily or weekly, and check in with each other as an additional way to encourage new healthy habits.

 INSPIRATION

In his book *The Omnivore's Dilemma: A Natural History of Four Meals,* Michael Pollan writes:

Imagine if we had a food system that actually produced wholesome food. Imagine if it produced that food in a way that restored the land. Imagine if we could eat every meal knowing these few simple things: What it is we're eating. Where it came from. How it found its way to our table. And what it really cost. If that was the reality, then every meal would have the potential to be a perfect meal. We would not need to go hunting for our connection to our food and the web of life that produces it. We would no longer need any reminding that we eat by the grace of nature, not industry, and that what we're eating is never anything more or less than the body of the world. I don't want to have to forage every meal. Most people don't want to learn to garden or hunt. But we can change the way we make and get our food so that it becomes food again—something that feeds our bodies and our souls. Imagine it: Every meal would connect us to the joy of living and the wonder of nature. Every meal would be like saying grace.

#24

COMMIT TO AN EXERCISE PLAN

Regular exercise makes you more efficient—and happier.

Physical fitness is not only one of the most important keys to a healthy body, it is the basis of dynamic and creative intellectual activity.

—JOHN F. KENNEDY

Your body doesn't need only fuel. It also needs exercise—and exercise isn't only a way to burn calories, strengthen muscles, and make ourselves look more attractive; it also lowers blood pressure, makes our hearts healthier, and improves the quality of our lives in all sorts of ways. When you feel good physically, Best-Day-Ever living becomes a whole lot easier.

When we think about the health benefits of exercise, we often focus on the "physical" versus the "mental." As we stressed in Strategy #22, your brain is part of your body. Researchers have found that our mental firepower is directly linked to our physical activity. Regular exercise improves concentration, sharpens memory, helps us learn faster, gives mental stamina, enhances creativity, helps us cope with stress, and elevates mood.

So why aren't we all out there exercising every day? The most common answer is: "I don't have time." Everyone knows how that feels. Life is so full. It's hard to make time for one more thing. But when you say to yourself, "I don't have time for that," what you're really saying is, "That's not a priority for me."

We *make* time for the things we consider priorities, even on our busiest days. For most of us, basic physical hygiene is a priority—so we very seldom say, "Oh, I just don't have time to brush my teeth today." If we're parents of young children, feeding them is generally a priority too; under normal circumstances, we'd never say, "Sorry, kids, I'm just too busy this week to make you dinner. You guys are on your own until I get this project done." We also make time to talk to our friends, buy groceries, eat meals, and clean up the kitchen. If we considered exercise to be as much a priority as all these things, then we'd find ways to move our bodies every day. We wouldn't even think about it; we'd just do it.

Here are six strategies for making exercise a regular part of your life:

1. ***Do physical activity you genuinely enjoy***, something you look forward to doing. If you find exercising on a treadmill boring, for example, consider going for a walk around the neighborhood instead. Or, if you have a favorite TV show, watch it when you're on the treadmill (and ONLY when you're working out if you want extra motivation). If you

enjoy sports, then sign up for a team or join a gym. But it doesn't have to be a sport, if you're not an athlete—just find some enjoyable way to actively move your body. If you do, you'll be much more likely to make it a regular part of your routine. The best exercise is the one that you'll do consistently.

2. ***Don't think of exercise as a chore.*** Think of it as something you are doing for yourself. Focus on the benefits that exercise gives you (such as feeling happier and more alert or becoming stronger so you have more endurance). My mood dramatically improves when I exercise routinely, so that's something that motivates me. Exercise is so effective at mood stabilizing that the American Psychological Association recommends it as a mood enhancer and even an effective tool to help with depression.

3. ***Set yourself goals for improving your performance.*** Research has shown that "mastery goals"—which psychologists define as goals to achieve new levels of competence—increase people's ability to follow through on exercise plans. One of my tricks for kick-starting physical fitness is to sign up for a race (any race: a triathlon, zombie run, half-marathon, etc.). The act of paying for the entry fee coupled with the time-imposed deadline is highly motivating. Just competing with yourself pays dividends too. Besting your own record and being able to see steady gains engages your interest and keeps you from getting bored. It will also give you small milestone "wins" to celebrate. According to Charles Duhigg, author of *The Power of Habit: Why We Do What We Do in Life and Business,*

"Once a small win has been accomplished, forces are set in motion that favor another small win." Each small win helps convince you that bigger achievements are within your reach, fueling your enthusiasm and self-confidence.

4. ***Make a financial commitment to your exercise plan.*** Hire a coach, enroll in a course you might never try (for me, that was rock climbing), prepay for an unlimited month of classes at a boutique gym, buy yourself the right clothing and equipment. The sense of investment will make you more likely to follow through. If I have signed up for a class and paid for it ahead of time, I will always go because I hate losing money. Consider that you are saving over $2,500 per year in health and medical costs when you get healthy and stay healthy. It's true! A study done by the *Journal of the American Heart Association* found that just thirty minutes of moderate, deliberate activity per day, five days a week, reduced medical costs by $2,500 per year.

5. ***Exercise with friends.*** Socializing while you exercise makes it more fun—and if you have a commitment to meet a friend at a certain time to walk, play tennis, or go to the gym, then you're less likely to find excuses to back out. Join a team that will count on you to be there. The power of community and friendship is strong. Studies are clear that people who have close ties and close friendships live longer and live happier lives—and exercise can be a part of that. I have a group of active friends that I go hiking with, others that I run with, and some that I do Pilates with. I make sure that I'm seeing a friend to work out with, usually

about two times a week. This helps me take care of my friendships and my own body at the same time.

6. ***Multitask.*** Raking leaves, walking the dog, vacuuming, and shoveling the driveway are all ways to move your body. It's okay to kill two birds with one stone by getting something done around the house or yard at the same time that you're exercising. Be conscious and intentional about ramping up your movement, though. Don't assume that it will happen by itself.

What works for me won't necessarily be what works for you—so find what does work for you! However you do it, make a plan to move your body every day.

 BUSINESS APPLICATION

Exercise done *during* the workday improves your productivity. Research from Leeds Metropolitan University found that busy professionals who exercised during the day not only felt more productive, but they were also less likely to lose their temper with colleagues or respond impulsively to stressful situations. They had more energy in the afternoons, when they otherwise typically experienced a "post-lunch dip" in productivity and focus. They went home at the end of the day feeling happier and more satisfied with their day. The type of exercise didn't matter, and neither did the length of the exercise period. No matter what form of exercise the workers engaged in or for how long, they all got the same effects.

Instead of viewing exercise as something you don't have time for because it takes you away from work, consider physical activity as a necessary part of a normal workday.

 MAKE IT PERSONAL

Reread the six methods I suggested for making exercise a regular part of your life. Pick one that appeals to you most. How will you implement it in your life this week?

- At the end of the week, take time to evaluate how well you kept to your plan. What worked for you? What didn't?

- After moving your body regularly for a week, did you notice any changes in the way you felt, both physically and emotionally? Did your sleep patterns or mood change? Describe any changes you notice. (Writing down the positive effects of exercise will help you to remember and be more motivated.)

Are you willing to commit to making this a part of your weekly plan from now on? If not, try another method and see if that works better for you. Also consider integrating exercise with the food journal I recommended in Strategy #22. There are apps available that can help you do this. A simple habit tracker app that's currently available is Habit Share.

 INSPIRATION

In *The Power of Habit: Why We Do What We Do in Life and Business,* Charles Duhigg indicates that forming an exercise habit is one of the best habits you can build for yourself. "Typically," he says, "people who exercise start eating better and become more productive at work. They smoke less and show more patience with colleagues and family. They use their credit cards less frequently and say they feel less stressed. Exercise is a keystone habit that triggers widespread change."

You're in Charge

PART IV

You're in Charge!

Claim and use your power.

#25

HAVE AN INTERNAL RATHER THAN EXTERNAL LOCUS OF CONTROL

Believe that you act upon the world, rather than the world acts on you.

Many complaints are made of the misery of life;
and indeed it must be confessed that we are subject to calamities . . . .
But surely, though some indulgence may be allowed to groans
extorted by inevitable misery, no [one] has a right . . .
to [feel] debarred from happiness by such obstacles
as resolution may break, or dexterity may put aside.

—SAMUEL JOHNSON

As Samuel Johnson said back in 1751, life has miseries and calamities that make us complain and groan—but we have the mental power and the skills to rise above these obstacles. It's easy to forget that we have the option to do that. Instead, we allow ourselves to believe that we're powerless in the face of circumstances. We give away our control.

In personality psychology, locus of control defines how much people believe they are ultimately responsible for their own successes and failures. If your sense of what controls your life, your *locus* (Latin for "location") of control, lies within yourself, then you feel you have personal power over your life. If your locus of control is external, then you feel that your success and happiness are determined by things outside your control. People who have a strong internal locus of control believe that their efforts and abilities will eventually lead them to success; when they experience setbacks, they see them as opportunities to learn and gain new strengths. People whose locus of control is external, however, believe that their success or failure, happiness or sadness, is outside their control and is dependent on luck, other people, or the environment into which they were born. They do not see how their own actions—or lack of action—could be at the root of their happiness and success. As Pulitzer Prize-winning author Alice Walker said, "The most common way people give up their power is by thinking they don't have any."

EXTERNAL LOCUS OF CONTROL	INTERNAL LOCUS OF CONTROL

The outcomes of your life are outside your control. Fate, other people, your environment, or other factors shape your life.	The outcomes of your life are within your control. Your hard work, decisions, and skills have the power to shape your life.

None of us is totally one thing or another—we're all somewhere on a continuum between a totally inner locus of control and a completely external locus of control—but the more we recognize where our attitudes place our control, the more we'll be able to shape new habits of thinking that will empower us. Pay attention to the things you catch yourself thinking.

For example, do you say to yourself, "I'd like to exercise regularly—but I just can't because my workdays are too long, or my kids are too young, or I can't afford a gym membership, or I'm too tired"? (I'm familiar with these excuses because I've used them all at one time or another!) These kinds of thoughts place your locus of control outside of yourself. It says that you have no power to make a choice to be healthier because circumstances have already made that choice for you. Telling yourself, "Exercise is a priority in my life, so I am going to walk during my lunch hour, or get on the exercise bike while my kids nap, or get up twenty minutes earlier and go running," shifts your locus of control so it's inside you now. It gives the power back to you.

One of my first lessons in this principle came during my third year in business running a retail store. Like many small business owners, I discovered that running a retail store is harder than it sounds. The store had recently transitioned from the manager who got the store off the ground to an experienced retail-store manager who had big plans for franchising our little creativity makerspace. We dreamt big in our meetings; it was exciting to draw up plans for a kiosk that could go into any mall. The normal day-to-day stuff with the store (opening, closing, cleaning, balancing the till) had to be done, even as we schemed on how to make our prototype Bellingham store into something big.

As the months went by, however, the wheels of progress seemed to be slowing. Lots of big ideas were being generated and some mall feasibility visits took place, but business and behaviors at the retail store started seeming inconsistent and spotty. There were a few reports that the store didn't open on time or that the manager had been bellicose or rude at work. It started going downhill so fast and far that I was seriously considering letting the manager go—as soon as I could get to it.

During all this conflict, Bramble Berry's chief operating officer (the person who runs the warehouse, makes sure packages get out the door, keeps the lights on at the warehouse) and his wife were having their very first child, so I was needed at Bramble Berry to help augment the role the COO would normally be doing; it didn't seem like a good time to do a major personnel change at the retail store. As a result, things at the store were left to run on their own, with very few checks and balances. After all, who had the time? I was trying to manage a warehouse and shipping operation.

Then, on the last day of my COO's paternity leave, I got an e-mail from the store manager that went something like this: "The money is gone. I guess I wanted you to fire me." And then he didn't come to work and open the store. I scrambled, got the store opened, and sent the COO and my business coach out to the manager's house, where they found him drunk and rambling incoherently. He threw them some very old checks written out to the store, rambled some more, and, by that afternoon, he had hired a lawyer. And so had we.

When the dust settled and the books were cleared, it was apparent that there was a discrepancy between what we *should* have had in the bank account and what we *did* have in the bank account. I was beside myself. It wasn't the money—though, of course, I wanted and needed that money—it was the broken trust. I had sat in on meetings, dinners, lunches with this manager. He was a friend. Yet he had stolen from me.

I put into practice a few of the strategies in this book, in particular the Power of the Trudge (A Deeper Dive in Strategy #5) and Choosing to be Optimistic (Strategy #7), but in order to be successful at any of them, I first needed an internal rather than external locus of control. It would have been easy for me to blame everyone else for the embezzlement and theft. After all, I didn't put my hand into the till and steal the money. I didn't delay the bank deposits and take the checks home to my house so I could try to wash the ink off and rewrite my own name on them. But that kind of thinking wasn't productive. It didn't help me move forward past the crisis. Instead, my COO and I examined our roles in the debacle. We examined our own culpability in what had happened. Then, we took charge of what we could by putting a stronger system of checks and balances into place for future managers, and we moved forward confidently from a place of trust. We gave control back to ourselves, instead of handing it over to the manager who had ripped us off.

Don't wait for a big crisis to build an internal locus of control. Make it a habit now, when confronting all of life's smaller frustrations.

It takes practice, though, to notice when your locus of control is slinking out the door. Say you're caught in a traffic jam for half an hour. Do you find yourself thinking, "This is terrible! I'm going to be so late. I hate this! Why do I have such terrible luck?" Of course, it's really not about your personal luck, because there are about a hundred other people sitting there caught in the same traffic jam—and when you let that delay put you in a bad mood for the rest of the day, you've handed your personal power to a traffic jam. Instead, you could reclaim your power by saying to yourself, "Well, while I sit here waiting, I'm going to listen to that new podcast I've been waiting to have time to hear." Or you might use the half hour you're sitting there in some other creative, productive way that transforms the delay into a gift of unexpected time.

Locating that pesky locus of control is a little like playing "Where's Waldo," but you can learn to recognize the telltale signs. Listen to yourself when you describe your life. Do you say things like "I'm overwhelmed by my life" or "My life is spinning out of control?" The favorite one I find myself uttering way too often is: "I'm so busy!" The reality is that I schedule myself and my family, so if "I'm so busy" is true, whose fault is that? I've tried to replace that phrase with "Life is full," which puts the power to change the situation firmly back in my court.

Another clue to locating your internal locus of control is if you find yourself experiencing the same set of negative circumstances over and over again. For example, maybe you keep falling in love with people who end up breaking your heart; or year after year you lose out on the promotion you hoped for; or you get sick several times a year because you're working too many hours and not nourishing yourself properly. All these things could indicate that you've let your control slip out of your hands, that you've allowed yourself to become a servant of circumstance rather than a stronger person who uses her inner power to shape her life.

Locus of control is shaped in part by our background. If you grew up with parents who continually emphasized your personal responsibility, then you may just naturally have a stronger inner locus of control. On the other hand, if your parents continually blamed external factors—such as their social status, their education, their health, or their finances—for their success or failures, then you're more likely to have a stronger external locus of control. But this is one more chance to take control, even of your locus of control! You don't have to sit back and say, "Oh well, my parents taught me to be like this, so now there's nothing I can do about it."

A lot of research has been done around locus of control. Social scientists have found that having a strong external locus of control makes people more prone to depression, alcoholism, and obesity—while people with a strong inner locus of control are less vulnerable to depression, do better in school, cope better with stress, are more satisfied with their jobs, and are more oriented toward achieving their goals.

Of course none of us can control all the circumstances in our lives—and that means we all experience days (weeks, months) that are more crappy than happy! For example, in the year after our house blew up, our son Jamisen started exhibiting some odd eye movements. We attributed it to a post-traumatic stress reaction. After all, the kid had been through a lot in a few short months! After a few months, though, the movements were so distracting that he couldn't focus on anything for long. We took him to eye doctors. They were mystified. Then we took him to his pediatrician. She looked at his movements and referred him to a pediatric neurologist in town, because, in her opinion, he appeared to have the same movements as focal-point epilepsy. Initially, we were stunned and devastated by the potential diagnosis. But after the initial (and very normal) stages of stressful emotions, we took a deep breath and chose how we were going to react to that news more constructively. We channeled our emotional energies into making a written plan of action, and we started problem-solving quickly. The pediatric neurologist referred Jamisen to Children's Hospital, and after two long days there and countless tests, we got to the bottom of the mystery—a much-less-serious eye issue. Finally, with the help of medication, his symptoms have mostly disappeared.

When we run into events like that—a child's illness, a business deal going sour, a serious car accident, a friend's betrayal, or any of the other catastrophes life brings along—we can choose to focus on the actions that *are* within our control. That means we ask ourselves, "Given these circumstances, what can I do next? What action can I take? What choices can I make?"

Other people's reactions are some of the things we can't control, and neither should we try to. Remember, though—you do control whether you surround yourself with toxic friends, impossible work environments, or unhealthy romantic relationships. You also control how much effort you put into your profession, your relationships, and your physical and emotional health. You can act upon the world, rather than waiting for the world to act on you.

You have power—so use it!

BUSINESS APPLICATION

Research reported by Michael Kolacz, a professor of management at Davenport University, found that an internal locus of control aids businesspeople by helping them to be:

- more self-motivated
- happier and less stressed
- better in control of their individual behaviors
- more active in seeking information
- better problem-solvers
- better able to handle complex information
- more creative

- better able to demonstrate initiative and independent action
- more likely to assume or seek additional leadership responsibilities

 MAKE IT PERSONAL

To assess where your locus of control is hiding out, answer these questions as honestly as you can.

1. Do you believe the good things that happen to you are due mainly to luck or chance?

2. When something doesn't turn out the way you had hoped, do you blame others?

3. When you are upset, do you feel like your emotions are out of your control?

4. When you have a disagreement with someone, do you find yourself thinking over and over about what the other person did wrong?

5. When you run into a problem or challenge, either with work or in a relationship, do you want to give up or run away?

If you answered "yes" to most of these questions, then you may have a strong external locus of control. If you answered "no" to most, then you probably have a stronger internal locus of control.

- What are three things in your life right now that you feel as though you can't control?

- For each of these three things, list positive actions you could take that would give you greater control over the situation. It's okay if they are small actions. Any action will help you to regain your internal locus of control, even if it's only in a small way.

 INSPIRATION

At the 2016 Olympics in Rio, eighteen-year-old Yusra Mardini was the flag-bearer of the Refugee Olympic Team. A year earlier she had almost died in the Aegean Sea while escaping by boat from war-torn Damascus to Turkey. When the small boat began to sink with nearly twenty people on board, Yusra and her younger sister jumped into the water and pushed the boat to shore, swimming for three hours. Her faith, courage, and swimming skills saved her life and that of the other people who were with her. "I could not drown," she said at an Olympics press conference, "because I am a swimmer and I had a future to pursue."

Developing her talent as a swimmer was challenging in Syria. Yusra said, "Sometimes we couldn't train because of the war. Or sometimes you had training but there was a bomb in the swimming pool."

Yusra clearly has a strong inner locus of control! "When you have [a] problem in your life," she said, "that doesn't mean you need to sit down and cry like babies. The problem was the reason why I am here, and why I am stronger."

#26

ACCEPT RESPONSIBILITY FOR YOUR LIFE

*Don't surrender to victimhood—
use whatever power you have.*

*Inner peace begins the moment you choose
not to allow another person or event
to control your emotions.*

—PEMA CHODRON

Recently, when I was facilitating a discussion group, I posed the question, "What's an experience you've had in your life that knocked you down and you came back stronger?" We went around the room, telling our stories. When it came my turn, I said, "When I was sixteen years old, I was caught in an 8.2 earthquake on Guam." I then went on to tell what happened.

I'd been staying with friends of my parents, helping out with housework and taking care of the family's eight- and twelve-year-olds. One day the parents went out to dinner, while I stayed with the kids. As I drove to pick up some groceries, the pavement in front of me suddenly buckled and then rose up and down. Two little boys riding in the back of the pickup truck in front of me were nearly bounced out onto the road. I turned the car around and drove as fast as I could back to the house.

When I got there, I found that the driveway had moved several inches away from the road. I rushed into the house, calling the children's names. Every single cabinet in the house had fallen over, and broken glass was everywhere—but the children were safe.

I was worried about the gas lines—was everything going to blow up at any minute?—so I got the kids out of the house, and we all climbed into the family's car. That tiny compact car felt like the safest place to be right then. I put the car in gear and drove slowly through the ruined world, looking for the kids' parents.

Guam is a small island, and I knew where they'd gone to have dinner. The kids and I made it to the restaurant, where we found more devastation. Every single bottle behind the bar had crashed onto the floor, every plate and glass on the tables had smashed. We picked our way through the broken glass and china, and found the kids' parents, crouching under a table.

"Okay," I said to myself while rapidly making a to-do list in my head, "we found the parents. Now we have to clean the house. Right? Now we have to make the house habitable. Okay. Now how are we going to get water? How are we going to get light? Where are the flashlights? Start looking now!"

The next three days were spent with all of us cleaning up the mess and trying not to worry about aftershocks. Thinking about that period in my life still washes a wave of emotion over me, but at the time, I felt very focused. I had to make sure the children were safe, and then I had to take the next step—and then the step after that—on my list . . . until, little by little, life went back to normal.

That was a very scary experience for a teenager. I learned very quickly that ordinary life could suddenly, without any warning, fall apart. You could be safe one moment and in terrible danger the next. After the earthquake, I could have curled up and hidden, terrified to venture out. The experience might have made me afraid for the rest of my life.

Instead, I learned that even in the middle of a disaster, there are choices you can make. This goes back to having an internal locus of control, like we discussed in Strategy #25. But what I learned during that earthquake went further. I realized that thinking like a victim puts the focus completely on yourself—and you end up paralyzed with fear. The opposite response, however—accepting responsibility to do whatever you can—turns you outward. It empowers you to act.

At the most practical level, that means that today I'm probably the only person in Bellingham, Washington, who bought earthquake insurance *before* buying insurance for fire or theft. I have a disaster planning preparedness kit with dried food, a camping stove, and a LifeStraw water filter. I do all those things not because I've let my life be controlled by fear, but because I'm determined that, no matter what happens, I'm going to do whatever I can to take care of my family. While I can't do anything to prevent a natural disaster, there *are* things I can do should a disaster happen, and I accept responsibility for those things.

So back to the discussion group and the question I'd asked: "What's an experience you've had in your life that knocked you down and you came back stronger?" Everyone in the room had something meaningful to say—until it was Martha's turn.

"There has not been one single experience in my life that has made me stronger," Martha said. "It's all just knocked me down, and I could never get back up, and it just kept knocking me down further and further." She stared around the circle at us, as though challenging us to contradict her.

Martha has had three failed marriages, her health is poor, she's given up on managing her weight, and she's admittedly miserable. I've been around her enough to know that, no matter what you say to her or do for her, she takes it as an insult or an opportunity to argue or complain.

In truth, however, Martha's life experiences were no more challenging than anyone else's in that room. In fact, as a white woman who had received a sizable inheritance, she probably has had more advantages throughout her life than most people. But Martha can't see that. In her own eyes, she's a victim. Because she refuses to accept any responsibility for her own happiness, her victimhood has frozen her in place. As a result, she's having her *worst* day ever—every day.

We all have a little Martha inside us—that tiny person within our heads who stomps her feet and says, "It's not fair! Why can't people be nicer to me? I shouldn't have to do this! I give up!" But we don't have to listen to her.

We can't keep terrible things from happening—but we *can* be responsible for how we respond to them, and we can choose to take constructive action. The power is within us!

BUSINESS APPLICATION

Joshua Margolis, a professor of Business Administration at Harvard Business School, has collected research on how businesspeople can face challenges head on, building a repertoire of skills that allows them to recover quickly and respond constructively to hardships.

Sinking into victimhood, says Margolis in an article published by Harvard Business School, is counterproductive. It doesn't clean up the workplace mess. He suggests that businesspeople build themselves an "adversity toolkit" that will help them quickly take responsibility in a crisis. "Write it down," is one of the tools he recommends; if you describe the problem on paper, it may prevent you from spinning your wheels complaining to your colleagues. Psychologists have found that the act of writing allows us to distance ourselves from our emotional responses to circumstances. As part of that, says Margolis, it's important that you first recognize your emotions and name them—and then step back from them. Take a few deep breaths; focus on a happy memory or a joyful thought; and then ask yourself, "What could I do now?" Margoli's research indicates that when people are asked what they *could* do, they are more likely to come up with ideas than when they are asked what they *should* do.

Margoli says it's also helpful when professional adversity strikes to think about the situation from four perspectives:

1. **Control**: Where and how can you take responsibility? Then, work with your team or colleagues to identify all the areas where you can have an impact.

2. **Ownership**: Regardless of your job description, how can you step up to make the most immediate and positive impact on the issue?

3. **Reach**: How serious do you think the problem is? How far will its influence reach? Then think of something you can do to reduce the size of the problem. Baby steps count, says Margoli (remember A Deeper Dive: The Power of the Trudge, in Strategy #5!), so even if you can come up with something that improves the situation by just 10 percent, that's progress. Consider the strengths and resources you and your team or colleagues can develop by addressing the issue.

4. **Endurance**: How long do you think the situation will last? Think about what you'd like the business to look like on the other side of the obstacle. Consider what you can do in the next four hours to move in that direction. Develop a series of steps and an ongoing process for dealing with the setback.

MAKE IT PERSONAL

- The table below shows traits that are more responsible and those that are less responsible. Which characteristics do you identify with most?

MORE RESPONSIBLE	LESS RESPONSIBLE
Internal Locus of Control	External Locus of Control
Focusing your thoughts and attention	Letting your minds drift aimlessly
Thinking through alternatives and consequences	Relying on habit or taking the easy way
Learning from past experiences	Blaming past experiences on others
Fulfilling your obligations to others	Evading obligations
Opening to new ideas and information	Being stubborn and closed-minded
Accepting responsibility for error	Refusing to acknowledge responsibility
Being adaptable and flexible	Needing to have everything the same, refusing to change
Being able to do things independently	Being dependent
Seeking solutions	Assigning blame
Participating	Bystanding
Talking *to* people	Talking *about* people
Saying things like, "I choose to . . ." or "I decided to . . ."	Saying things like "I had to . . ." or "I had no choice . . ."
Believing in your own power	Believing you are helpless

- Describe an experience you have had in your life that knocked you down but in the end made you stronger.

- Describe a situation in your life right now that is difficult or challenging. What emotions do you feel when you think about this set of circumstances?

- Despite the difficulty of the situation, what are two things you could do this week that would make things better? Where can you take responsibility (which will help you shift your locus of control back inside you)?

 INSPIRATION

Best-selling author Dean Koontz grew up in a cold, cramped clapboard-and-tarpaper house with an abusive alcoholic father. Instead of becoming a victim of his background, however, even as a child Dean found a way to gain control of his own life through reading. "Books were an escape from the violence of the household and the poverty," he said in a *Publisher's Weekly* interview. "They showed me different worlds. A writer was the greatest thing you could be." Then he started writing his own stories, because, he said, it took him "out of that awful house." Even as a child, he was taking responsibility for his own happiness.

As he grew up, he kept writing, refusing to let his circumstances turn him into a victim. Success did not come quickly or easily, but he still kept going. He published his first book in 1968, but it wasn't until eighteen years and fifty-eight books later that he hit the bestseller lists.

"He just kept at it, and kept at it," said Irwyn Applebaum, president and publisher of Bantam Books. Dean took responsibility for his life, working seventy or more hours a week at writing his books. Today, his books have sold more than 200 million copies and have been translated into thirty-three languages.

"Fairly early," he said, "it became obvious to me that you could take anything that happened to you in one of two ways: You could be depressed by it, or you could be motivated by it. That's been reinforced by everything I see in life . . . . I was born as poor as it gets, tarpaper shack sort of house and no money coming in, violence, alcoholism, everything weighted against me. But there were always people in my life who were there, to teach me something worth learning or to support me . . . . So I look around and say, 'How can I not be an optimist?' And I am, I'm a raging nut-case optimist."

#27

CHOOSE YOUR FRIENDS

Be intentional about the people you spend time with.

If you hang out with chickens, you're going to cluck,
and if you hang out with eagles, you're going to fly.

—STEVE MARABOLI

If I could give my twenty-year-old self some more advice, here's what I would say: "You know all those friends you have now? Well, some of them I'm still best friends with today, and I find value and inspiration in their company. And some of them drifted away as we grew apart. And you know that one friend you love to binge watch DVDs of *90210* with? The one you love to chow down on Doritos and Oreos with, while neither of you get out of your sweatpants all day? She's not good for you—and you're not good for her.

"And I have to tell you, I'm glad I outgrew that phase. I wish I'd outgrown it a sooner. If you don't want to turn into the habit, quit hanging out with the person who enables the habit. Hang out with people who drive you to be better, who you admire, and who lead lives that you would be proud to trade with. So go outside, twenty-year-old self, take the sweatpants off, and make some new friends."

My twenty-year-old self may have had a lot still to learn—but today I'm grateful for the friends I have and the way in which they help me live my Best Day Ever. Here's an example of the kind of conversations we have:

"Hey," I'll say, "you know that condo I've owned for years that we've been renting? Oh my goodness, there's black rot and black mold in it, and it turns out that the black mold is in the beams of the condo, so now it's structurally unsound. And our renter's gone. Doesn't that suck?"

"Yeah, that sucks," they'll all say—but then they'll help me turn it around, even though I just unloaded my unhappiness all over them.

"Okay, now let's come up with something positive you can focus on," one of them says.

"I wonder if they can upgrade for earthquake retrofitting when they put in the new beam?" another friend says.

"Hey," adds another, "this is a good opportunity for you to paint the place. You've been saying you've wanted to for a few years now."

"Once you do all that work," yet another friend tells me, "I bet you'll get another renter that you like better. And then you'll be able to recoup all the money you're losing now."

When I leave my friends, I go home feeling encouraged. I'm no longer upset. They have helped me push my locus of control back inside me where it belongs (Strategy #25). They have helped me see where I can step up and take responsibility (Strategy #26). They have reminded me that I can choose to be optimistic (Strategy #7).

Imagine how I'd be feeling, though, if my friends had responded differently, if we'd spent the next hour complaining about how badly life sucks, making each other feel worse and worse. We'd start complaining next about our jobs, and our husbands, and other friends not currently present. It would feel good at the time, all that complaining to people who understand exactly how I feel, but by the time I went home, I'd be in a worse mood than when I started. We would have created a pile of negative energy, and that never does any good.

The world is full of interesting things that make better topics of conversation than gossip and whining. As Eleanor Roosevelt said, "Great minds discuss ideas; average minds discuss events; small minds discuss people." Talk about books, talk about the latest TED Talk, talk about things that you're brewing up in your life. Inspire each other, challenge each other. Help each other be the best versions of yourselves. Nudge each other into using the strategies in this book. That's the kind of friendship you need in your life.

But there are likely people in your life whom you genuinely love but who help feed your negativity (and vice versa). Maybe they're family members or old friends who seem like family. For whatever reason, you don't want to walk away from these people. So what do you do?

I have a friend with whom the only thing I'd ever done for decades was go out to eat, talk, and drink wine. We'd meet for dinner, we'd drink wine, and we'd discuss the politics and news of the week. It was a vibrant, fun friendship built on a foundation of food, wine, and smart conversation. There's nothing so wrong about having a nice dinner, stimulating discussion, and some wine, right?

Except we both realized that drinking so much wine was getting in the way of the Best-Day-Ever life we wanted to be living. So last year we decided to quit drinking wine for thirty days. Great. We were excited. But then we looked at each other. "What are we going to do together," I asked, "if we can't drink wine?"

She was silent for a minute, and then she said, "I have an idea. Let's train for a half-marathon."

She wasn't a runner. I wasn't a runner. But we wanted to spend time together, outside of a restaurant. So we started training for a half-marathon together—and now she's my hiking and running buddy. She's no longer my wine-tasting buddy.

If you and your close friends have worn a rut that's not helping any of you, talk about it. Change up your habits. Try something new. Go to the gym in the morning with them instead of going out to eat at night. Instead of having them over to watch TV and eat Oreos, go on a hike. Learn salsa dancing with them. Find a new hobby, or learn a new skill together. If you change the circumstances under which you typically engage with them, then you'll find that will automatically shift the unhealthy patterns. You'll add positive energy to your relationships to replace the negativity.

If you and your friends are truly close, you should be able to enlist each other's energy to help each other grow. For example, all of us gossip sometimes; it's a destructive habit that can be terribly seductive, so address it with your friends intentionally and deliberately. Make a pact to catch each other whenever you start gossiping. A friend and I have done that, because we know so many of the same people that it's easy to start out talking about something innocent and then gradually slip into the kind of conversation that is really just talking behind someone's back. So whoever notices what's going on first says, "Hey. Why don't we change the subject? So, what book are you reading?"

Of course, not everyone will be open to recognizing when elements of a friendship have become negative. In that case, you may not be able to talk to them openly about the changes you want to make in your relationship—but if you can change your habitual patterns of interaction, they may not even notice that you're deliberately steering conversations away from negative topics and moving them toward gratitude and abundance and big ideas.

Sadly, there are some people, though, who are just too happy wallowing in misery for you to be able to do anything to change them. They feel comfortable in the mud and the muck, so they're saying to you, "Hey. Come on in. The water's fine."

But when you join them down in their swamp hole, you realize, "Oh! This is muddy, disgusting water. Why am I here?" You don't want to get stuck down there with them, so you may need to gently and lovingly let them go. If they're happy where they're at, it's not your job to "fix" them, but at the same time you can't allow them to prevent you from building a life of health, a life where luck is something that you have created, where you are happy today and every day, and where you believe something good is going to happen each morning when you wake up. Not everybody wants to be there, and that's okay—but it doesn't mean you need to try to lug those people along on your back. The reality is that it's much easier to pull someone down than it is to pull somebody up. As Jim Rohn has said, you are the sum total of the five people you spend the most time with.

This also goes back to Strategy #25 and Strategy #26. Being intentional about your friendships puts your locus of control within you, rather than outside with negative people who want to share their negativity with you. It also means that you take responsibility for doing whatever you need to do to keep yourself healthy. This will require self-awareness. You'll need to notice how you feel after you've been with someone. Do you feel more creative, more able to tackle life's challenges? Or do you feel down on yourself, discouraged?

You don't have to be a victim of negative people. You have the power to make different choices.

BUSINESS APPLICATION

In a 2015 *Harvard Business Review* article, Emma Seppala and Kim Cameron connect building positive relationships in the workplace with productivity. They refer to a large and growing body of research that says that when people with positive relationships work together, they create a positive culture— and a positive culture leads to "dramatic benefits for employers, employees, and the bottom line."

Seppala and Cameron's research indicates that six essential actions contribute to building intentionally positive relationships that add energy and life to the workplace. These are:

- Caring for, being interested in, and maintaining responsibility for colleagues as friends.

- Providing support for one another, including offering kindness and compassion when others are struggling.

- Avoiding blame and forgiving mistakes.

- Inspiring one another at work.

- Emphasizing the meaningfulness of the work.

- Treating one another with respect, gratitude, trust, and integrity.

MAKE IT PERSONAL

Take a deliberate look at the friends with whom you spend the most time by filling out this chart:

FRIEND'S NAME	WHAT IS A TYPICAL ACTIVITY YOU DO TOGETHER?	HOW DO YOU TYPICALLY FEEL AFTERWARD?	ON A SCALE OF 0-5, HOW MUCH NEGATIVE ENERGY DO YOU SOAK UP FROM THIS PERSON?	WHAT ACTION COULD YOU TAKE TO CHANGE THIS?

INSPIRATION

Cognitive science reinforces the concepts that underlie friendship choices of Strategy #27. A Harvard study that followed a group of men for seventy-five years found that strong relationships with friends was the most important factor contributing to long-term well-being. Not only can friendship make us healthier and happier, but it also makes us more successful in other ways as well. Students who had close friends in college earn more when they grow up than young people who didn't have good friends. Ultimately, we absorb qualities from the people we spend the most time with. Per a 2015 *USA Today* article by Ted Fishman, "Smarter friends make us smarter; more social friends make us more outgoing; healthy friends make us more health conscious. Who they are becomes part of us."

#28

BE THOUGHTFUL ABOUT YOUR EXPOSURE TO MEDIA

Garbage in, garbage out.

The difference between where you are today
and where you'll be five years from now
will be found in the quality of books you've read.

—JIM ROHN

I only want to put things into my head that support the life I want to live and the person I want to be. This means I'm careful about the media I expose myself to. I don't want to spend my time with negative people (Strategy #27)—and I don't want to spend my time immersed in anything else that's negative, either.

This means that I have actively chosen not to watch TV. Why would I want to lose myself in someone else's fantasy life when I can create a life that I love? So I use my evenings, after the kids are in bed, for reading books that teach me in one way or another, and for meditating, doing yoga, and connecting with friends who lift me up and give me energy. I don't sink down on the sofa and mindlessly absorb whatever the TV is dishing up. Instead, I create a life that I don't want to take a vacation from, that I don't *need* to take a vacation from. That only happens because I choose what goes in my brain, rather than allowing it to become a passive receptacle.

I don't turn on the news in the car, and I don't watch the news on TV. (Full disclosure: We don't even have a TV that's hooked up. I didn't grow up with one. My husband didn't grow up with one either. A match made in heaven, right?) The news is designed to be sensationalized, using other people's pain and suffering to increase ratings and keep people hooked. Most "news" is as good as gossip. Why would I want to let that garbage in?

This doesn't mean I've shut myself away from the "real world." I read magazines that inform me without fear mongering. I subscribe to online news amalgamators that keep me up-to-date without force-feeding me a heaping helping of negative energy. I pay for subscriptions to the *New York Times* and *Washington Post* and read them regularly. I use the Internet to also keep up with the popular shows people are watching, like *Orange Is the New Black* and *Game of Thrones,* because I'm happy to occasionally connect and talk about the ideas that can be pulled out of the latest episode. I just don't want to consume hours' worth of someone else's values, fantasies, or feelings of hopelessness every evening.

I've found that a better use of my energy is focusing on the small things I *can* do to help make the world a better place (the things I can take responsibility for, like we talked about in Strategy #26). I could choose to volunteer with the Red Cross' Home Fire Preparedness program. Or I might work on the homelessness issue by carrying small "necessities" packs in my car to hand out, little bags with a power bar, clean socks, and, for women, sanitary napkins or tampons. The opportunities are everywhere you turn—but you'll never see where you can take on responsibility for making a practical difference in the world if you're just sitting in front of a TV, soaking up all the sadness and violence and fear that's out there.

Say you're regularly watching a TV show where the main character with whom you closely identify happens to be having an affair. At the subconscious level, how much more comfortable are you going to get with the idea of being sexually unfaithful to your spouse? A lot more comfortable? A little more comfortable? Just enough to push you over the edge at your next business trip after you've had that second glass of wine?

Mindlessly cramming the wrong input into your brain is like typing incorrect numbers into a calculator and then expecting the calculator to give you a correct answer. If you fuel your mind with fear, then you're not going to be filled with optimism (see Strategy #7, Choose to Be Optimistic). If you take in a constant diet of shallow entertainment, then you're not going to have room in your head for your own new ideas and creativity.

It's a simple fact that there is only so much time in a day and, as we've previously discussed, time is a precious resource to use wisely. At the end of your life, would you rather look back and realize you spent a gazillion hours watching television or skimming through Facebook—or would you rather look back with pride and happiness at the master's degree you earned, the hours you volunteered, the projects you completed, and the uplifting books you read? Bill Gates once said, "I really had a lot of dreams when I was a kid, and I think a great deal of that grew out of the fact that I had a chance to read a lot." Look where reading the right kind of books got him!

Don't kid yourself, though: Novels and magazines aren't necessarily any better than television and the Internet, just because we've all been trained to think that reading is a good thing. I have a friend who recently realized that reading murder mysteries had become her automatic fallback whenever she felt tired. "I'm exhausted, I don't want to do anything, I don't want to cope with the world," she'd say to herself, "so I'm just going to curl up and read this murder mystery and that's okay. It's like taking a little vacation from life. And that's a good thing sometimes." But she came to realize that her appetite for murder mysteries was like a craving for potato chips or Oreos; satisfying that craving felt good in the moment, but afterward she didn't feel less tired or more able to deal with her life. Her reading wasn't nourishing her mind and spirit.

That's become my criteria, the benchmark I use for evaluating whether I want to expose myself to a particular piece of media: Does it nourish me in some way? Does it inspire me to handle my life better? Does it open me up to new ideas? Does it teach me something I need to know? Does reading this allow me to later produce something of greater value than if I hadn't consumed it in the first place?

Even with that philosophy, I confess that I still enjoy some reading material "snack food" now and then—I just try not to binge! I keep up with pop culture by reading some of the popular books of the day through a neighborhood book club. I also happily pick up a gossip magazine or two to read on the plane for business trips. Sometimes it gives my brain a much-needed break and at other times I'm left feeling like I just gorged on a dozen deep-fried Twinkies.

Media is like friendship: we wouldn't want to do without either in our lives, but we need to be deliberate about the choices we make. The Internet, books, and all the other forms of media out there can be amazing, wonderful sources of information and ideas. They can change our lives. They connect us to other thinkers, past and present, and they allow us to learn from the entire human community.

If you want to outpace everyone else, read more than everyone else—but read things that teach you new things, whether that's fiction or nonfiction. Learning is the key to doing extraordinary things. No one starts out knowing how to run a company, travel the world, or be a great long-distance runner. There are people who have done all these things, however, and they've been so successful they've written books about it. Read those books. Put them into practice. Improve yourself by learning more and by learning faster.

And while you're at it—turn off the TV.

BUSINESS APPLICATION

In a 2015 *Harvard Business Review* article, Shawn Achor (author of *The Happiness Advantage*) and Michelle Gielan (author of *Broadcasting Happiness*) reported their research indicating the effect of media consumption on worker performance. Building on a Gallup study that found a close connection between professional productivity and emotional moods, Achor and Gielan divided study participants into two groups to determine how negative versus solutions-focused media affected their mood later in the day. One group watched three minutes of negative news stories before 10 a.m., while the second group watched three minutes of solutions-focused news, stories of resilience that support the belief that we have personal power (an inner locus of control) and that our behaviors can make a difference in the world. Then the participants were e-mailed six hours later and asked to fill out a survey that would indicate stress levels and mood. Individuals who watched just three minutes of negative news in the morning had a 27 percent greater likelihood of reporting their day as unhappy six to eight hours later.

Based on their research, Achor and Gielan have this advice to professionals who want to be happier and more productive:

Turn off news alerts: Since most news alerts are negative, try turning them off for one week. These alerts also pull our attention away from the present moment, which can lead to decreased work performance. "If there's anything really important happening," say Achor and Gielan, "you'll hear about it soon enough."

Cancel the noise: In the same way you might cancel the noise on a plane using headphones, meditation can help you tune out the emotional noise that's constantly bombarding us from multiple forms of media.

Change the ratio: Start your day with empowering, solutions-focused news. Seek out stories that offer action steps and potential solutions, instead of just focusing on the problems. "If you don't like that there's so much negative news," say Achor and Gieland, "don't forget: you vote with your fingers. Every time you click on a story, you're telling the media you want to be consuming this."

MAKE IT PERSONAL

- For the next week, keep a log of how much media you expose yourself to, using the chart below. Don't try to limit your exposure at this point; just do what you would normally do and then record it, along with how it affected your mood and whether you learned anything useful from it.

DATE	HRS. SPENT WATCHING TV OR MOVIES	HRS. SPENT READING	HRS. SPENT ON SOCIAL MEDIA	HRS. SPENT INTERNET SURFING	MOOD AFTERWARD ON SCALE OF 1 TO 5	DID YOU LEARN ANYTHING USEFUL?

- After keeping track of your media exposure for seven days, have you learned anything? Do you need to reduce the time you spend on media— or do you need to change the type of media to which you're exposing yourself? What are three things you can do differently next week?

INSPIRATION

The World Economic Forum says that the right kind of book can change the world in positive ways. It lists the following nine examples of novels that impacted readers so strongly they were inspired to take action:

Uncle Tom's Cabin, by Harriet Beecher Stowe, brought the horrors of slavery to the attention of the public on a personal level for the first time, causing an uproar that eventually led to Emancipation.

The Jungle, by Upton Sinclair, sparked a public outcry over food hygiene, which led to the formation of the US Food and Drug Administration (FDA).

All Quiet on the Western Front, by Erich Maria Remarque, exposed the horrors of World War I and triggered anti-war movements.

Things Fall Apart, by Chinua Achebe, revealed the impact of colonialism on African culture and identity.

The Ragged Trousered Philanthropists, by Robert Tressell, was an integral part of the drive for social reform at the start of the last century.

The Grapes of Wrath, by John Steinbeck, brought the world's attention to Depression-era poverty and the destitution of hundreds of thousands of migrants making the journey to California to find work.

1984, by George Orwell, provided a timeless reminder of the importance of freedom of thought and speech.

To Kill a Mockingbird, by Harper Lee, continues to give generations of readers a valuable lesson in looking at the world through another person's eyes, promoting tolerance and fighting racism in the process.

Beloved, by Toni Morrison, reveals the long-term legacy of slavery.

Reading the right kind of book can inspire you to take responsibility (Strategy #26) to do what you can to make life better for others.

#29

GO WITH THE FLOW

Be adaptable to whatever life brings.

The only way to make sense out of change
is to plunge into it, move with it, and join the dance.

—ALAN W. WATTS

I went to the gym a few weeks ago and found that the group exercise room was under construction. I was bummed since I was there for Zumba (which, in my humble opinion, is basically the most enjoyable class in the entire planet). I said to the woman standing next to me, "Oh that's a bummer, I guess I'll go hit the treadmill."

She responded with a scowl and growled, "They didn't even notify us! I hate this place!" Then she stomped off.

She actually left the gym rather than change her workout plans! Numerous thoughts went through my head, but those that really struck me were that she wasn't very committed to her workout if she was willing to leave because of a minor setback—and she wasn't very flexible and able to roll with the punches.

Going with the flow becomes even more vital when you suffer larger disappointments on your way to living out your mission. Being thrown off your plan—or off your game—doesn't necessarily mean disaster. It often ends up being just a detour to an even better outcome.

For example, there was the time that Obama stood me up. I had won the honor of being named Entrepreneur of the Year by the Small Business Administration for Washington State (one of fifty recipients for each of the states). I was thrilled, but it was a crazy time: I accepted the award and gave birth to my first child (via C-section) less than twelve hours later. Three weeks later, I was heading off with my husband and newborn to meet the president in Washington, DC.

Part of the award included the opportunity to meet President Obama, along with other winners from other states. While my body and common sense were shouting, "No way!" I nevertheless said, "Absolutely!" (after all, one of my bucket list items was to meet Obama in person). So off I went with my husband and newborn.

My belly still hurt, my legs were still wobbly, and I was a nervous wreck—our son, Jamisen, was teensy tiny, and there we were lugging him through airports—but we arrived safely at the White House, where all fifty winners milled around waiting for President Obama. Tiny Jamisen was wearing an American flag onesie, with red, white, and blue stripes on his little legs, the cutest little baby you'd ever seen.

And then we got the news that the president was dealing with an international issue. He had had to go across town to the State Department, and he wouldn't be back. I was crushed, and I couldn't help but feel that I'd put Jamisen and my traumatized body through all this for nothing.

Eventually, I pulled myself together and made up my mind to go with the flow . . . and things still worked out surprisingly well. In fact, better than I could have imagined. The award gave me more prominence in Washington State's business world and, as a result, the state governor, Jay Inslee, utilized me and Bramble Berry in a publicity campaign promoting Washington as a business-friendly place. This was great, free marketing for us!

The governor also invited me to several events. And guess what? One of the events was a private meet-and-greet with President Obama! Almost five years after the day when I was supposed to meet with him as part of a larger group, I was able to meet with him in an even more personal, one-on-one setting.

By going with the flow—instead of sinking into gloom and resentment—my ultimate experience turned out just fine.

Being adaptable is an essential skill to have in business as well as in life. Think about how many things (big and small) haven't gone your way just today. I'm willing to bet that, if you look closely and pay attention, you've already compromised or changed your plans at least fifteen times today. Maybe you couldn't wear what you had planned on wearing ("Whoops, that shirt's in the laundry"), your spouse couldn't drive the kids to school as planned ("What? You have an 8 a.m. meeting you forgot to tell me about?"), or a co-worker misunderstood you ("Huh? You thought I was doing that? I thought YOU were taking care of it!"). If you got bent out of shape and stomped off in frustration every time something went sideways, you'd be wasting a lot of time in your day.

The more efficient approach is to adapt quickly. Like everything else, learning to roll with the punches is a skill you can learn. Start small and build up.

Three ways to improve your flexibility are:

1. Come up with a mantra. When something doesn't go my way, or it's different from what I envisioned, I say to myself, "It is neither good, nor bad; it simply is." This reminds me not to judge the situation but, instead, to attach no value to the circumstances, trusting that something will work out.

2. Evaluate the options. There are always more than just two options. Unlike the woman at the gym, don't have it in your head that only *one* thing will make you happy. Train yourself to come up with three solutions to every course change or correction. This will train your brain to see the gray areas versus only black and white. Life is full of a lot more choices than you might think—and they're not all total win-or-lose options.

3. Take action and reevaluate. After you try one of your new options, reevaluate. How did it work out? What were the positives that came because your initial plan didn't work out? This will help you see that not everything needs to end the way you initially planned to be a success.

Take these three simple steps every time you are thrown for a loop, and it will soon become automatic. You won't think about it anymore, but you will find yourself grimacing much less when change happens. Your heart rate will remain normal when you experience setbacks, as you quickly and seamlessly adapt. You may even be able to see that there is adventure, opportunity, and even genius in the detour.

Going with the flow isn't just aimlessly wandering through life, letting "fate" determine what happens to you. You can go with the flow and still have an inner locus of control (see Strategy #25). You'll still have your big goals in place—but you will be willing to accept a new route to reach them.

BUSINESS APPLICATION

Mary-Anne McCarthy, Accenture New Zealand's technology lead, believes that it's important that you create a "go-with-the-flow" business culture— what she refers to as a "liquid" culture—and that you look for that quality and reinforce it in your employees. Flexibility and the ability to learn are becoming, she says, more important than traditional technical skills.

Because technological change is accelerating, you and your employees must be able to learn and adapt. If you can't, says McCarthy, you'll miss out on opportunities. "To have an agile business, you've got to have an agile workforce and that by defini-tion is the liquid workforce," she goes on to say. "If you think of liquid in its form, it can change to any shape, you can fit it in any mould, you can move it, it can flex and that's the fundamental thing that we see as the missing part of the transformation."

When it comes to marketing your business, going with the flow becomes even more essential. "The ability to adapt quickly to changes in consumer behaviour," says Dom Dwight, marketing director at Taylors of Harrogate, "such as the move towards shopping across discounters and traditional super-markets, or the growth of online shopping and the rise of social media—is vital as it requires brands to rethink how they present themselves to the world."

Ultimately, as Virgin Group founder Richard Branson has said, a company that can't go with the flow will soon be forgotten. "Every success story is a tale of constant adaption, revision, and change."

 ## MAKE IT PERSONAL

- Look back on the last week. Describe an occasion when events did not go as you had planned. How did you react? Were you able to go with the flow?

- I have another mantra I use pretty frequently to calm my mind when things start cascading the wrong way: "I love my life. My life feels good. Everything I want comes to me easily and effortlessly. I relax." What feels good to you? What could you say to put yourself in a different state of mind than panic, fear, or worry? Think of your own personal mantra that you will say to yourself when things don't go the way you had hoped. Write it down and keep it handy. (Remember, writing will help it to stick in your mind.) Practice repeating your personal mantra throughout the day, so that it comes easily to mind the next time life's currents push you in a different direction from what you had planned.

(Change your mantra as needed. I've had several variations of mine over the years.)

 INSPIRATION

Taoism has a word for a concept that's similar to "going with the flow"—it's called *wu wei* (pronounced "ooo-way"), which means "effortless action" in Chinese. Edward Slingerland, a professor of Asian religion, describes it for the *New York Times* as "that state of effortless performance sought by athletes, but it applies to a lot more than sports . . . . Wu wei is a complicated concept that is perhaps best explained by describing a stream flowing down a mountain. The stream is not consciously trying to do anything, but it is still active. Even when the stream encounters obstacles, it adjusts effortlessly and keeps flowing forward. If we can be like the mountain stream, then we will find that life is decidedly less stressful."

#30

ASSUME GOODWILL

Don't waste time and energy resenting other people.

There is a huge amount of freedom that comes to you when you take nothing personally.

—DON MIGUEL RUIZ

Here is another piece of advice I wish I could give to my twenty-year-old self: "Don't take other people's words and actions personally. It's *not* personal. No one is thinking about you. Quit thinking they are. They're all too worried about their own situations to be focused on you. So when you think someone has insulted you, not only did they probably not insult you, but they've most likely moved on to other things. Assume that they meant well. Then you're free to move on to the next thing and focus on how you're going to reach your goals."

Each time we get offended by something another person said or did, in effect we're making up a little story in our heads. Say you're walking down the street and you see someone you know. You call out, "Hi! I haven't seen you in so long! How are you?" The other person barely glances at you, and then he hurries on his way.

"That person just gave me the cold shoulder," you say to yourself. "How rude! What gives him the right to act like that? He could have had the courtesy to at least answer me."

When you get home, you're still fuming, so you call a friend on the phone. "I just ran into so-and-so," you say, "and do you know what he did? He was completely rude to me!" Then your friend and you talk some more about this other person, and you make the narrative about him a little more elaborate, because your friend tells you about another time this person did something similar to her. Together, you add on to this little story you've created and expand it. Later, you talk to your spouse about this person's rudeness to you. You find yourself still thinking about it when you go to bed, and you get upset all over again.

Look at how much time you gave to this person! You let him move into your head and live there rent free, and meanwhile you wasted hours of your time when you could have been planning a new project, enjoying your family, or doing something creative. That one tiny moment on the street has you pinned in place.

And all the while, you have no idea what the other person was actually thinking when he ignored your greeting. Maybe he was preoccupied with a serious problem that has nothing whatsoever to do with you. Maybe he didn't even hear you or see you. Or maybe he *was* being intentionally rude, because he has poor social skills, and he's never learned the rules of common courtesy. There are all sorts of scenarios to explain his behavior, none of which have anything whatsoever to do with you.

So don't take it personally. Tell yourself another sort of story to explain his behavior, a story where you don't feature as the main character. And then move on. Doing that frees you and allows you to move forward, building momentum toward your goals.

Practicing this on social media is especially important. Without the social clues we depend on in face-to-face interactions, people on Facebook, Twitter, and in chat rooms or forums easily take offense. They see insult and injury in every careless comment—so they respond angrily, creating an entire knot of negative energy that clogs communications. Don't let yourself get sucked in. Assume goodwill on the part of everyone concerned—and then let it go. Don't give it space in your head.

The next time someone says or does something that seems rude or hurtful, instead of getting offended, reframe what just happened. Say to yourself, "Wow, that was weird. She's not normally like that. Maybe she's having a bad day." Then give yourself a mental shrug and press on happily with your day.

 BUSINESS APPLICATION

E-mail and social media has transformed the business world's communication streams. It's a wonderful, convenient tool that we depend on so much today that it's hard to imagine how we ever functioned without it. But digital communication is not a perfect form of conversation.

Have you ever received an e-mail from a colleague or business associate that sounded curt and snippy? Or read a tweet that set you back a bit? The "tone" of the message made you feel upset and defensive.

You wondered what you did to make the other person angry. Those negative feelings can then get in the way of a constructive relationship.

Meanwhile, the person who sent the e-mail, tweet, or snap wasn't angry at all; he was just in a hurry. He knew he needed to communicate a message, but he didn't have much time to do it. Maybe he was between meetings. Maybe it was the end of the day and he needed to go home, but he wanted to make sure he sent that transmission before he left. There are all sorts of scenarios that could explain what you interpreted as a curt tone.

The dangerous thing about digital communication is that it can be easy to misinterpret the writer's emotions. We can't see the other person's expression or hear the tone of their voice. If we can assume goodwill, however, we won't let typed messages derail our working relationships. Instead, we can read each e-mail and digital broadcast we receive with the assumption that the other person means well and wants to work productively with us. That's a far more efficient way of doing business!

 MAKE IT PERSONAL

- Describe a recent experience when you felt offended by someone.

- What story did you tell yourself about the other person?

- Now reframe that story. Tell another one that assumes goodwill on the part of the other person.

 INSPIRATION

In Don Miguel Ruiz's book *The Four Agreements: A Practical Guide to Personal Freedom,* the second agreement is: "Whatever happens around you, don't take it personally." Ruiz goes on to say:

Nothing other people do is because of you. It is because of themselves.

All people live in their own dream, in their own mind; they are in a completely different world from the one we live in. When we take something personally, we make the assumption that they know what is in our world, and we try to impose our world onto their world . . . .

Even when a situation seems so personal, even if others insult you directly, it has nothing to do with you. What they say, what they do, and the opinions they give are according to the agreements they have in their own minds . . . .

As you make a habit of not taking anything personally, you won't need to put your trust in what others say or do. You will only need to trust yourself to make responsible choices. You are never responsible for the actions of others, you are only respon-

sible for you. When you truly understand this and refuse to take things personally, you can hardly be hurt by the careless comments or actions of others.

If you keep this agreement, you can travel around the world with your heart completely open and no one can hurt you. You can say I love you without fear of being ridiculed or rejected. You can ask for what you need. You can say yes or you can say no— whatever you choose—without guilt or self-judge- ment. You can choose to follow your heart, always.

Build habits that focus on the positive.

Gratitude unlocks the fullness of life.
It turns what we have into enough, and more.
It turns denial into acceptance,
chaos to order, confusion to clarity.

—MELODY BEATTIE

In 1944, the Nazis captured Elie Wiesel, his parents, and his three sisters, along with thousands of their Jewish neighbors in Sighet, Hungary. They were put into cattle cars and shipped off to concentration camps at Auschwitz, Buna, Birkenau, and Buchenwald. At Auschwitz, Elie was separated from his mother and sisters, but he and his father stayed together.

On his first night in Auschwitz, Elie saw German soldiers throwing Jewish babies into a fire, and in the months that followed, he witnessed hangings, escaped the human ovens, and endured the hatred of the Nazis. After a year at the camp, he had to stand by and watch while his father died from dysentery and starvation. Elie decided he no longer wanted to live in a world that was so terrible—but, nevertheless, he survived. After he was liberated from the concentration camp, he grew up to be one of the world's most beloved authors.

In 2000, Oprah Winfrey interviewed Elie Wiesel and asked him, "Despite all the tragedy you've witnessed, do you still have a place inside you for gratefulness?"

"Absolutely," Elie answered. "Right after the war, I went around telling people, 'Thank you just for living, for being human.' And to this day, the words that come most frequently from my lips are 'thank you.' When a person doesn't have gratitude, something is missing in his or her humanity. A person can almost be defined by his or her attitude toward gratitude." He went on to say, "For me, every hour is grace. And I feel gratitude in my heart each time I can meet someone and look at his or her smile."

Gratitude—feeling and expressing appreciation for what you have—is more than a nice, virtuous attitude. Gratitude is what allowed Elie Wiesel to move beyond the horrors of his past and transform them; it gave him the strength to become someone who helped make the world a better place for others. And gratitude is one of the strategies that's most essential for building your Best Day Ever.

 And that's a scientific fact. Studies show that people who intentionally cultivate gratitude heighten their sense of well-being and happiness. They also increase their physical and emotional energy. They have a greater sense of optimism (see Strategy #7) and more empathy for others. Research shows that gratitude can even strengthen our immune systems.

Gratitude has long-term as well as short-term benefits. One study found that people who, daily over the course of one week, wrote down three things for which they were thankful were then significantly happier for the next six months. According to other studies, people who regularly practice expressing their gratitude feel a greater sense of abundance in their lives, are more aware of life's small pleasures, experience less depression, are kinder to others, and have fewer complaints about the people in their lives. Research also indicates that gratitude can improve romantic relationships, increasing happiness and understanding between partners.

Gratitude not only makes *you* happier, but it also improves the lives of those around you. People who hear regular expressions of gratitude feel better about themselves. They're kinder. They're more willing to be helpful and go out of their way to do things for others.

Like so many of the Best-Day-Ever strategies, gratitude is something that increases and becomes stronger the more you deliberately practice it. Two of the tools that the research has found most useful for cultivating gratitude are writing thank-you letters and keeping a gratitude journal. Making one or both of these practices part of your routine will create "gratitude ruts" in your brain. The act of writing (preferably by hand) will make these thoughts stick in your mind better. Gradually, gratitude will become habitual.

Bad things happen in life. We all have catastrophes and crises. Gratitude gives us greater resilience for dealing with negative events. Instead of getting ourselves stuck in the doom-and-gloom muck, we're able to bounce back more quickly and move on.

 MAKE IT PERSONAL

- Over the next week, come up with at least three things (or, if you really want to challenge yourself, five things) each day for which you are grateful and write them down. No repeats allowed!

- At the end of the week, take a few minutes to think about how you feel about your life now that you've spent seven days focusing on gratitude. Do you feel more positive? What changes did you notice in your physical and emotional states? In your relationships?

If you notice that gratitude has had a positive effect on your life, consider extending this exercise by keeping a gratitude journal for another thirty days. After a month, you may find that you want to make this a permanent part of your life.

Another practice that can help you cultivate gratitude is taking five minutes every morning, before the start of your day, to meditate on the things in your life for which you are grateful. You might want to try this exercise: As you inhale, say, "I am grateful for . . . ," and as you exhale, say, "I let go of my negative feelings about . . . ." By doing this at the beginning of the day, you program your brain to respond more positively for the rest of the day.

#31

CHOOSE YOUR THOUGHTS

Reframe your mental conversations.

You need to learn how to select your thoughts
just the same way you select your clothes every day.
This is a power you can cultivate.

—ELIZABETH GILBERT

Many people (perhaps even most) don't seem to think they can choose their thoughts. They believe they have no way to shape their own mental activity, as though it were a force of nature, something beyond their control. "Well, of course I'm upset!" they say. "He made me angry and totally ruined my day." Or they get caught up in self-criticism: "Why am I so dumb? I keep making the same mistakes. I might as well give up because I just never change."

Psychologists tell us, however, that we don't have to be at the mercy of our thoughts. Thoughts can become habitual, granted, but we have the power to form new habits of thinking. It just takes conscious determination.

Think of your mind as being a little like a radio. Let's say you have two stations you can choose to tune into: "This day is the best day ever," or "Wow, this day is hard." Both stations are real; they're each playing a version of the truth. We can be aware that these two stations exist, but we can't play them both at the same time. In other words, we can only think one thing at a time; we can't have two thoughts that are actively happening at the same time. We can't say to ourselves, "I am so happy about this day," while we're also somehow moaning, "This is the worst day ever." Since you can't tune into both messages at the same time, here's where you have power: You get to choose which one you want to listen to.

In his book *Change Your Brain, Change Your Life*, Daniel Amen says, "every thought sends electrical signals throughout our brain . . . and they can impact every cell in our body, making us feel either good or bad." Amen goes on to say that even though our thoughts are "real"—in the sense that they have physical effects—they are often wrong. In that case, it's like you're tuning into a radio station that's broadcasting lies.

Those radio stations are constantly on the air, chattering away from the moment we wake up until we fall asleep. We're so accustomed to the background noise in our heads that we often don't realize that there are constant mental conversations broadcasting in our minds—and, as it turns out, *we* are the radio announcers! Just as we can choose which words come out of our mouths, we can also choose which words we think.

So how do you do this? First, you'll need to pay attention. Notice the words and sentences that are playing in your mind. If you find yourself feeling depressed or upset, for instance, then look at the thoughts that are running through your head. Odds are good you're thinking something negative. "Why did he do that to me? He's so unfair!" "I messed that up so bad. I'm such an idiot!" "Nothing ever works out right. What's the point of even trying?"

To counteract thoughts like these, you'll need to deliberately shape different thoughts. Psychologists refer to this as "reframing self-talk," and you do it by consciously talking to yourself, replacing the old negative thought habits with new ones. When I run into a difficult situation, for example, I make a practice of saying to myself, "I am 100 percent in charge of my response to this situation." This leads to a pause that's followed by: "So how am I going to choose to respond? What action can I take? How can I change this situation?"

Reframing your thoughts is a vital part of living your best day every day. It has a positive effect not only on your emotions but also on your relationships, your professional success, and your productivity. Research has found that retraining your thoughts can contribute to an increased life span, lower rates of depression, greater resistance to the common cold, reduced risk of death from cardiovascular disease, and better coping skills during hardships and times of stress.

Reframing your thoughts strengthens your inner locus of control. It's a way to claim your own power to choose your life. And the more you do that, the more habitual it becomes.

BUSINESS APPLICATION

A study reported in a 2016 *Business Insider* article found that positive "self-talk" improves people's success levels when doing work. Here are some examples of positive statements that the researchers found improved performance:

- *I can do better next time.*

- *I can do this.*
- *I can handle this.*
- *I'm making progress.*
- *I can get even more done tomorrow.*

 MAKE IT PERSONAL

For the next few days, practice listening in on your own thoughts. Notice when you're playing a negative "radio station"—and jot down the thoughts that are playing. List a few examples of your recurring negative self-talk.

Sometimes these may be very old thoughts that have been playing a long, long time, ever since you were a child. But just because they've been around for so long doesn't mean they're true—or useful. In fact, these thoughts are probably keeping you from Best-Day-Ever living.

Now, for each negative statement that you wrote, write a sentence that reframes it positively. The following chart gives some examples of how you might reframe them.

NEGATIVE	POSITIVE
This is a problem.	This is an opportunity.
This is too complicated for me.	Let me tackle this from a different angle.
I made such a terrible mistake—I never do anything right.	I can learn from this mistake—and I'll do better next time.
I don't have what I need to do this.	Necessity is the mother of invention.
There's no way this will work.	I can try to make it work.
I'm just too lazy to get much done.	I can't fit everything into my schedule, but I can reexamine my priorities.
There's no point in trying when I've already failed.	I'll give it another try and see what happens.
That's too risky.	Let's take a chance.
This is too hard.	This is a challenge.
This is terrible.	This is a growth experience.
Life is always such a struggle.	Life is always an adventure.

Consciously make a habit of thinking these positive thoughts. Whenever you catch yourself listening to that negative radio station, switch the station. Reframe your thoughts. You have the power to choose what you think!

INSPIRATION

A Cherokee story tells about an old man who says to his grandson, "Each of us has a battle between two wolves going on inside of us. One wolf is angry, envious, sorrowful, greedy, and arrogant. He is full of self-pity, guilt, resentment, and a sense of inferiority right alongside false pride. He constantly tells lies, and he hurts everything around him. The other wolf, however, is joyful, peaceful, loving, generous, and kind. He is full of hope, humility, and compassion. He always tells the truth, and he makes the world a better place for everyone."

"Do I have those wolves inside of me?" the grandson asked.

The old man nodded. "The same wolves are inside you—and they are constantly fighting with each other. They are fighting inside all of us."

The grandson thought about it for a minute, and then he asked his grandfather, "Which wolf will win inside me?"

The old man replied, "The one you feed."

#32

USE "ANCHORS" TO KEEP YOU POSITIVE

Create habitual statements to counteract negativity.

If you correct your mind,
the rest of your life will fall into place.

—LAO TZU

Recently, American Express decided to drop my company credit limit by almost 70 percent, and they also called my entire balance due the same day, both without any warning. This was not a happy surprise!

Besides the practical aspects of figuring out how to pay the money, emotionally and mentally I needed to process all this as well. It would have been easy to throw a pity party and fire off an angry letter to the CEO of AmEx. I did one of those things for about twenty-two seconds before I realized it wasn't helping me move forward. So then

I started reframing in my head, "Oh my gosh. How amazing it is that I even have this issue? Who would have thought, twenty years ago, that I even would be racking up bills like this because I would have a company this large? I'm so lucky. I'm so blessed." By the end of that little pep talk, my reality was that I was lucky and I was blessed. All of that had been true before the line of credit was called and it was still true afterward. The fundamentals of my life had not changed.

My internal pep-talk practice is deliberate. I've cultivated this habit to help me deal with life's frustrations, both the major ones and the trivial ones. I call it *anchoring*. By intentionally framing a positive counter-response, I maintain my inner locus of control (see Strategy #25). I don't allow myself to be swamped with negativity.

I have a few standard anchors that I use. One of the ones I use most frequently is: "Twenty years ago, I wouldn't have had this situation because—" If I have a problem with an employee, I think to myself, "I'm so lucky! Twenty years ago, I didn't even have employees." When the roof at Bramble Berry was torn off in a spectacular windstorm, after dealing with emergency roofers and cleaning fragments of roof from the neighborhood, the team and I talked about how lucky we were. "Oh my gosh! That could have been so much worse! Those roof fragments could have damaged a car in the neighborhood. Thank goodness for insurance to help us fix the roof. And can you believe we even own this building? I couldn't have even dreamed of owning a warehouse twenty years ago." That is my formula for many situations: "Twenty years ago I wouldn't have even had this problem because my life wouldn't have been as abundant as it is now."

Another useful anchor is considering what other people's lives are like. It is easier to get into a state of gratitude when you consider the plight of people who are suffering all over the world due to lack of resources, war, and famine. By comparison, my life is always blessed, no matter what the irritation of the day is. There is a phrase that pops up frequently on Twitter that is trite—but true: "I woke up today. I am blessed. You woke up today. You are blessed."

Another anchor I use is, "I can solve this." Instead of being angry about a situation or blaming other people for causing it, I see what I can do to fix it. It could be a small situation; for example, when I came into work the other day, I noticed that the flowers in the pots surrounding our office building were drooping. My first thought was: "This is so irritating. Those flowers cost good money. Why can't someone remember to water them?" My second thought was: "I can solve this."

The immediate solution was easy—it took me about five minutes to water the plants. And while I did it, I threw in a few more anchors for good measure: "I'm so lucky to have a building that I own that has flower pots around it. I wouldn't have had such a luxury twenty years ago. And I have clean water readily available to water these plants—when much of the world doesn't even have drinking water. Wow. I am so blessed. And every day I get to walk by these flowers and see such beauty."

And then, in a positive frame of mind, I went inside and found a long-term solution by asking, "Hey, you guys, who loves gardening in here?" When someone raised her hand, I said, "Okay. I have something for you to do. Would you like to be in charge of keeping these plants alive every single day?" Her face lit up; she was delighted to have a new job responsibility that enabled her to exercise her love of gardening—and get paid while doing it!

The examples I've given so far have to do with life's minor frustrations. But anchoring can help you better cope with major tragedies, as well. Recently, our daughter was diagnosed with an interesting medical condition called "tortuous colon." It is not life threatening, but it is something that has required some serious medical detective work, persistent parenting, and coordination between lots of moving medical targets. We have traveled to see specialists, had multiple procedures, and continue to work toward a solution for our toddler. My husband and I were both initially scared and worried, but we anchored our emotions by saying, "We're so lucky that we have the best medical care. Oh my goodness, we're so grateful that we have access to top-notch doctors." After the diagnosis, we also anchored by focusing on our gratitude for our child's life; her condition is treatable. There is always something or somebody that is worse off than you, and so there's always something to then be grateful for.

In Strategy #5 A Deeper Dive (Power of the Trudge), I told about the time when my house was uninhabitable because the boiler exploded. My biggest anchor at the time was this: "My family is safe! No one was hurt! Even if we don't have a house, we're all together, and that's all that really matters." The boiler was directly below my daughter's crib where she was napping. If the explosion had gone straight up, she might not have survived. Our son had left the playroom not ten minutes before the explosion blew out the walls and shot furniture and toys like projectiles through the room. Instead, miracle of miracles, the explosion initially shot sideways. We lost our wine cellar, play room, and all the furniture in the house—but not our daughter who was sleeping directly overhead or our son who had been directly in the path of the blast just ten minutes earlier.

I don't use anchors like these because I'm such a good person that I automatically see life's silver linings. I find anchors because I know that otherwise my knee-jerk reaction is to focus on the frustration. I'd be thinking, "This isn't fair. This is horrible. This is unbearable." I'd stomp around and get mad, damaging my relationships and taking up time that could be better spent doing something productive and creative. Or I might sit and cry, when I could be doing something positive to put the situation back together. Using anchors has become habitual now, but only because I was deliberate about writing down and rehearsing anchor statements ahead of time in my mind, so they'd be handy when I needed them most.

Anchoring can help you be happier with your life, but that's not its greatest value. The real value of anchors is that they give you the stability you need to take action. The anchor isn't the end goal. Instead, the anchor helps you be able to keep working toward your goals, even in the most discouraging circumstances.

 ## BUSINESS APPLICATION

Researchers have found that focusing on the positive aspect of every situation improves entrepreneurs' decision-making abilities. When you focus on the negative aspects of a situation, your decisions are more likely to be reactive, driven by emotion rather than by rational thinking.

You might think that focusing on the positive could also skew decisions, but instead, studies show that when you're in a positive frame of mind, you're more likely to find creative and constructive solutions. In *Understanding the Entrepreneurial Mind*, authors Alan L. Carsrud and Malin Brännback state that "negative thinking from entrepreneurs in a negative mood could lead to decisions which are more likely to be poor for their venture."

MAKE IT PERSONAL

- Think of a negative situation in your life that is going on right now. Then come up with your own anchor to hold you steady despite these circumstances. Write it down.

- You might also want to write your anchor on a note card that you tape to the dashboard of your car, to your bathroom mirror, and/or your computer. Repeat the anchor often, so it comes to mind easily when you need it most. After using your anchor for several days, note any changes you recognize in yourself, your attitudes, and your actions.

INSPIRATION

In 1913, a book was published that became an immediate bestseller: *Pollyanna,* by Eleanor H. Porter, which tells the story of eleven-year-old orphaned Pollyanna Whittier who plays the "Glad Game." The goal of her game is to "find something about everything to be glad about," whether it's a boring assignment or a lifelong illness. Pollyanna uses the game to spread cheer to her grim aunt, as well as everyone with whom she comes into contact, including a self-pitying invalid, a grouchy old miser, and an orphaned boy.

Pollyanna's game was born when her missionary father's request for a secondhand doll for Pollyanna resulted in a pair of crutches instead. Seeing his daughter's disappointment, Rev. Whittier suggested that they look for a reason to be glad about the crutches. Eventually, they decided they could at least be glad they didn't *need* the crutches, because that meant their legs were strong and healthy.

In the century since Porter's book was published, the name "Pollyanna" became shorthand for an obtuse (and annoying) cheerfulness. *The American Heritage Dictionary* defines a "pollyanna" as "a person regarded as being foolishly or blindly optimistic."

But the Glad Game is more than blind optimism. Pollyanna isn't always cheerful—she cries over disappointments large and small—but her game is a strong and practical tool that she uses to make herself happy. Her gladness is not a state of mind but rather a skill that became stronger with practice. "When you're hunting for the glad things," Pollyanna says, "you sort of forget the other kind." Learning the Glad Game doesn't only make the other characters in the book happier; it also inspires them to take positive action—to change their lives and the lives around them for the better.

#33

SURRENDER PERFECTION

The need to be perfect can paralyze you.

Instead of waiting for perfection,
run with what you got, and fix it along the way.

—PAUL ARDEN

Have you ever noticed that toddlers never worry about being perfect? When their first words aren't understood, they just keep trying to talk, getting a little better at it every day. When their first steps end with them falling on their faces, they get up and take more steps, until eventually they're walking—and then running. They don't worry that people will think they're stupid if they don't get things right the first time. They're not afraid they'll be rejected if they don't do something perfectly.

But somewhere along the way—about the time that we started school—we started thinking that being perfect really matters. Perfect worksheets were the only ones that earned gold stars and then 100s.

Falling short of perfect sometimes brought us scoldings from teachers and parents—and laughter and teasing from our peers. We started to internalize the message: "I need to be perfect." And pretty soon this morphed into, "I don't want to try if I can't do it perfectly." As perfectionists, our lives turned into an endless report card where our accomplishments or appearance earned either bad grades or good grades.

This attitude is sometimes reinforced by people who advocate for perfectionism as a way to motivate us to reach our goals. Psychologist Paul Hewitt, however, thinks this kind of thinking is unhealthy. After more than twenty years of research, he and his colleagues have found that perfectionism correlates with depression, anxiety, eating disorders, and other mental health problems, including suicidal thoughts.

The desire to be perfect, says Hewitt, is not the same as the generally healthier desire to excel.

What makes perfectionism so toxic is that it makes us focus on failure rather than success. Instead of being excited about our goals, we're frightened that we won't achieve them. We become too scared to step outside our comfort zones, because we don't want to risk looking stupid by falling on our faces. Our thoughts become obsessed with negatives rather than positives.

When I was young, I was overly driven to achieve perfection because I was insecure about my own value. I thought I needed to be good at everything I did to be loved more, to be accepted more. That changed for me after my first marriage failed. That experience was not only a personal heartbreak for me but was also the worst public humiliation I had ever experienced. I felt ripped to shreds, my failure exposed for everyone to see. The only people who were left in my life were the ones who genuinely liked me for me, not for the things I could do. As a result, when I put my life back together, my need for perfection lessened over time until it pretty much evaporated (though I still need to be aware of and monitor the tendency).

The fact is, perfectionism usually just gets in our way. Mark Zuckerberg at Facebook has realized this, which is why he encourages everyone to deliver new software releases quickly with the phrase, "Done is better than perfect." Unless you're a neurosurgeon or a person with a deeply technical job where lives depend on you (say, a pilot or a bridge builder), that is generally true. Forget the embarrassment of being just a teensy bit wrong and get out there, deliver something to the world, and improve on it once it's out. Don't fall into analysis paralysis and never put anything out because it won't be good enough.

Mastery doesn't just "happen." Malcom Gladwell wrote in his book *Outliers* that it takes 10,000 hours to get good at anything. Gladwell based his statement on research done by Anders Ericsson—and Ericsson has since qualified Gladwell's famous remark by stating that his research actually showed that there's no magic number for greatness; 10,000 hours was the *average* time that elites in their field had spent practicing their skills, but some practiced for much fewer than 10,000 hours and others for more than 25,000 hours. The point, however, is clear: it takes time to reach mastery. To expect anything less of ourselves is simply unrealistic.

When you watch people try to learn a new skill—be it a new language, a new musical instrument, or just a new computer program at work—it's always repetition that drives the mastery. No one is good at anything when they first start out. The moral of the story? Just start!

Toddlers have their Best Day Ever every day because they aren't hung up on the need to be perfect. They're delighted to keep trying because that's the extent of their world: trying, walking, falling. Over and over again.

We should learn from their example.

BUSINESS APPLICATION

Author and business coach Elizabeth Lombardo offers five tips that will help you counteract perfectionism in your professional life:

1. **Understand that done is better than perfect.** Perfectionists have a hard time finishing what they start. Because "perfect" is the only thing that's good enough for them, they never complete projects. Counteract perfectionism by following through to the end, no matter what.

2. **Use obstacles to your advantage.** Perfectionists tend to say, "Since this isn't working, maybe it is a sign that I should just give up." They view obstacles or mistakes as complete failures. Counteract perfectionism by realizing that roadblocks are not indications that your plan is flawed but only that more creative thinking is needed. When things don't go the way you want, assess the reasons why and use that information to adjust your course.

3. **Delegate.** Perfectionists say, "I have to do it myself or else it won't get done. I have no time to find someone to help me out and train them; it

is just easier to do it myself." Counteract perfectionism by realizing that if you try to do everything yourself, you will impede your success. Take time to find and train a team that will allow you to use your own time and energy wisely.

4. **Take breaks.** Perfectionist believe: "In order for my business to be a success, I need to work on it all the time. I'll take a break when I get my work done. I can sleep once I finish this project." Counteract perfectionism by understanding that, when you take care of your needs as a human being, your business will flourish.

5. **Focus on what you want rather than what you don't want.** Perfectionists say, "I should be more profitable. I do not want to fail." Counteract perfectionism by being motivated by passion rather than fear. Fear of failure can be powerful in the short term, but it also leads to stress, burnout, and business failure. When you have a true purpose for your business, you are more engaged and resilient, and ultimately, you're more successful.

 ## MAKE IT PERSONAL

Are you a perfectionist? Take the following quiz to see. Choose the best answer to each question. Be as honest with yourself as you can. If you're not sure of an answer, ask a good friend or your spouse what they think.

If you're working on a project and you realize time is running out and your deadline is coming up fast, do you:

1. Do the best you can to complete the project on time, even if it's not perfect.

2. Keep working as carefully as before and finish the job late—but to your original high standards.

3. Throw up your hands and quit, because there's no way you'll be able to finish on time.

Do you procrastinate if you're assigned an important but difficult task?

1. No, I'm always eager to get started with a new task, and I love a challenge.

2. Yes, because I'd rather be doing something easier.

3. Yes, because I'm so scared I won't be able to do it that I can't make myself get started.

If you find you're not very good at something, you:

1. Keep trying because you know that, although it may take a while and you may never be great, it's still fun to learn something new.

2. Give up and focus on something you're good at instead.

3. Give up because it's too hard and then feel terrible about yourself.

What do you tend to notice most when you look at a project that you've completed?

1. I focus on all that I did right, and I take pride in that.

2. I see all the things I can improve, and I get to work to make changes.

3. I get depressed because all I can see are the mistakes I made.

What do you tend to do when you look at a project that other people have completed?

1. I focus on the high points of their work, and I praise them for their accomplishment.

2. I see the mistakes they've made, all the little imperfections, and I challenge them to make their work even better.

3. I get depressed because I know I could never have done such a good job.

What do you tend to do when you look in the mirror at yourself?

1. I notice all the things I like about myself, and I don't worry about the rest.

2. I notice all the things I need to change about myself, and I make a plan to get my hair cut, lose weight, buy new makeup, or whatever.

3. I get depressed because all I can see are the things I hate about myself.

**Do people often tell you that
you're difficult to please?**

1.   No, I don't expect much. I'm content with whatever people can do.

2.   Sometimes, but I know I draw out the best in people, and that makes them feel empowered to become better people.

3.   Yes, people tend to think my expectations are too high or too rigid.

**What do you focus on most when
you're working toward a goal?**

1.   The process as much as the results. I enjoy the journey.

2.   The results. I always have my eye on the prize.

3.   All the things that could go wrong.

How do you feel if you fail at something?

1.   I don't like to fail, but I've found I can always learn something positive from the experience.

2.   I hate failure, so I avoid it at all costs. I work hard to avoid difficult situations where I might not be a success.

3.   I beat myself up over my failures. I get depressed, and I lose self-confidence.

**How do you feel if you receive
constructive criticism?**

1.   I am grateful for the feedback, even when it's not positive, because it helps me grow.

2. I feel angry and resentful. I get defensive and try to defend myself.

3. I feel upset, depressed, and hurt.

Now add up the numbers you selected (Example: If you chose option 2, that is worth two points). If your score is 10 to 14, you don't have much problem with perfectionism.

If your score is 16 to 22, you have a degree of perfectionism, but for the most part, your perfectionism inspires you to excel. Be careful, though, that it doesn't turn into a negative rather than positive habit. Become more aware of how perfectionism is affecting your life.

If your score is 24 to 30, perfectionism is getting in the way of how you live your life. It's robbing you of happiness, and it's holding you back from achieving all that you can. If that's the case, think of three "anchor" statements you can use the next time you recognize that perfectionism is blocking your path. (For example, "Even if I can't do this perfectly, I can be proud that I at least tried.")

 INSPIRATION

Author Brené Brown has this to say about perfectionism:

In the research, there's a significant difference between perfectionism and healthy striving or

striving for excellence. Perfectionism is the belief that if we do things perfectly and look perfect, we can minimize or avoid the pain of blame, judgment, and shame. Perfectionism is a twenty-ton shield that we lug around, thinking it will protect us, when in fact it's the thing that's really preventing us from being seen.

Perfectionism is also very different than self-improvement. Perfectionism is, at its core, about trying to earn approval. Most perfectionists grew up being praised for achievement and performance (grades, manners, rule following, people pleasing, appearance, sports). Somewhere along the way, they adopted this dangerous and debilitating belief system: "I am what I accomplish and how well I accomplish it. Please. Perform. Perfect." Healthy striving is self-focused: How can I improve? Perfectionism is other-focused: What will they think? Perfectionism is a hustle.

Last, perfectionism is not the key to success. In fact, research shows that perfectionism hampers achievement. Perfectionism is correlated with depression, anxiety, addiction, and life paralysis or missed opportunities. The fear of failing, making mistakes, not meeting people's expectations, and being criticized keeps us outside of the arena where healthy competition and striving unfolds.

#34

KNOW WHEN TO LET GO

*Don't hold so tightly to your goals
that you can't move on.*

The truth is, unless you let go,

unless you forgive yourself, unless you forgive the situation,

unless you realize that the situation is over,

you cannot move forward.

—STEVE MARABOLI

Remember Virgin Cola? How about Virgin Vodka? Virgin Cosmetics? Virgin Cars? VirginStudent (which was a lot like Facebook)?

If the answer is no, you're not alone. These early ventures of Richard Branson never got very far off the ground. In fact, they flopped, completely and utterly. And they weren't the only failed ventures Branson has on record. There's also Virgin Brides (wedding dresses), Virgin Clothing, Virgin Megastores, Virgin Pulse (an iPod competitor), Virgin Digital (similar to iTunes), Virgin Games, and

Virgin Lottery. Some of these ventures lasted a few years, some only a few months. But Branson never let their failure define *him* as a failure. Instead, he let go and moved on.

"My mother drummed into me from an early age that I should not spend much time regretting the past," he said in an interview. "I try to bring that discipline to my business career. Over the years, my team and I have not let mistakes, failures, or mishaps get us down. Instead, even when a venture has failed, we try to look for opportunities, to see whether we can capitalize on another gap in the market."

I haven't had a slew of failed business ventures, the way Richard Branson has, but I've had to let to go of plenty of things or change course over the years—my first marriage and that disastrous website company are just a couple of examples. If I hadn't been able to move on, I would have been frozen in regret, stuck in a never-ending mental loop of "if-onlys" and "what-ifs." The only way we can accept new joy and happiness into our lives is to make space for it by letting go of disappointments and might-have-beens. If our hearts are filled with pain and hurt, how can we be open to receiving new inspiration and recognizing new opportunities?

Psychologist John M. Grohol offers these steps for helping us to move on:

1. ***Make the decision to let it go.*** Things don't disappear on their own. You need to make a conscious commitment to let them go. Having an internal locus of control (see Strategy #25) will help you with this. You'll be able to see that the choice is yours; it's within *your* control.

2. ***Express your pain—and your responsibility.*** Talk to a friend. Write in your journal. Put your feelings in words, and then allow yourself to move past those feelings, to the place where you can take a more objective look at the

situation. By assessing your own contribution to whatever happened, you'll be able to learn from it and then move on with renewed energy and wisdom.

3. **Stop being the victim and blaming others.** This goes back again to having an internal locus of control, as well as accepting responsibility for your life (Strategy #26). You need to take responsibility for your own happiness, and not put that power into the hands of another person or thing.

4. **Focus on the present, the here-and-now—and joy.** When painful memories creep into your consciousness (as they are bound to do from time to time), acknowledge them for a moment—and then bring yourself back into the present moment. Some people find it easier to do this with a conscious cue, Grohol says, such as saying to yourself, "It's all right. That was the past, and now I'm focused on my own happiness and doing _____."

5. **Forgive everyone involved—including yourself.** Remember, forgiveness isn't saying, "I agree with what you did," and it's not a sign of weakness. Instead, it's simply saying, "I want to move forward in my life and welcome joy back into it. I can't do that fully until I let this go." According to Grohol, "Forgiveness is a way of tangibly letting something go." (This connects also to Strategy #30, Assume Goodwill.)

I recently attended a gathering of some of the top brand mavens in Washington State. With Seattle incubating some of the coolest, hippest brands in business, there were some heavy hitters at the table. I squeaked in because I knew the organizer. It was a heady dinner. The format was loose and easy: We shared a bit about ourselves, talked about what we wanted to do in the next year with our businesses, and then answered random questions. Maybe it was the great weather, maybe it was the glasses of champagne, or maybe there was something in the air—but before the first person was done talking, there were tears flowing. Because of that first speaker's vulnerability, all of us had permission to be honest about our lives and our businesses.

Everyone had a different story to tell, but many of them had to do with how we could know when it was time to walk away from something, whether it was a job, a business, or a direction. The conversations were enlightening. Here are some of the takeaways:

- It's okay to admit you're having an off week or an off month. Being in business isn't easy. But if you're not doing what you really want to do, don't keep pushing forward. If you have a nagging feeling that you made a mistake, then don't keep heading down the same road. Don't keep going in the wrong direction. Turn around.

- Sticking to a growth goal just because it's one you've invested in for years can have more to do with your need for control than it does courage and determination—and it can lead to failure. Know when to give up.

- If you love your business, but there's something about it that's getting in the way of your happiness, what can you let go of that will restructure your work so that you find more joy in it? Can you let go of the role you've always had to find another role that's a better match for your skills and passions? Are you willing to make drastic changes, no matter how frightening they are, to be true to what you believe is most important?

- Say "no" more often. When people ask you to take on extra responsibilities, you don't have to always agree. Be realistic about what you can handle and what's good for you physically, emotionally, and intellectually. Let go of the need to always please people. Surrender your desire to look competent and able to handle anything and everything.

- If something doesn't lift your spirits, do less of it. Of course, every business and every life has aspects that are boring or unpleasant, but don't let them consume your life. Those endless e-mails and the load of laundry will still be there in the morning—but you know what won't? Your kid's smile after he finally caught a football for the first time, or your daughter's grin as she takes her first step. People are fleeting—and more beautiful and amazing than any business goal.

- Let go of what needs to be released. This includes your need to be in control and be successful all the time, especially when it comes to achieving the perfect balance in your life. Some weeks are easy. Some are hard. Some weeks you feel like you're losing your mind. Other weeks, everything falls neatly into place. It's a teeter-totter. Don't ever expect to feel like life is perfect for longer than about two minutes. Don't make perfection a goal (Strategy #33). Be okay with life's ebbs and flows.

Ultimately, it comes down to this: Know when to let go. Let go of mistakes and failures. Let go of goals when they no longer serve you and the life you want. Let go of your need to impress other people. Let go of your urge to constantly be in control—and expect that there are some things you'll never be able to control. Let go of the past.

And once you've let go of all those things, you'll be free to move forward. Maybe your path will lead you in a new direction—or maybe you'll be able to go more quickly and joyfully in the same direction. Be willing to do either one.

 BUSINESS APPLICATION

Chris Kayes, a stockbroker and mountain climber, happened to be hiking in Nepal at the foothills of Mount Everest at the same time that the famous tragedy (described in the book *Into Thin Air*) took eight climbers' lives at the peak of the mountain. Kayes became fascinated with the psychology of the disaster that led these expert climbers to their death. The climbers who lost their lives had had clear goals, and they were determined to reach them—and yet the results were fatal.

Kayes realized that in the business world we often make the same mistake. We can see the summit—a lifelong goal is right there, seemingly within reach. Unfortunately, we're out of oxygen, it's getting dark, and a storm is brewing. We've become so identified with our goals, though, that the prospect of letting them go becomes unthinkable. We ignore evidence that should be pointing us in another direction, and instead we choose to invest even more in our goals. Stubbornly pursuing our goals in complicated, shifting business environments can lead us to disaster.

MAKE IT PERSONAL

- Spend some time taking an honest look at your life. What areas do you find the most frustrating? Where are the areas where you're unable to find much joy?

- Now consider: Is there something that's getting in your way in these areas? Is there something you need to let go of?

- Pick one thing from your list of things to let go. What can you do in the next week to begin letting go of it?

INSPIRATION

Lao Tzu was a Chinese philosopher who lived about 2,500 years ago—but his wisdom can still challenge and inspire us as we live our lives in the modern world. He has these things to say about letting go:

When I let go of what I am, I become what I might be.

By letting it go, it all gets done.

The world is won by those who let it go.

But when you try and try, the world is beyond the winning.

A good traveler has no fixed plans, and is not intent on arriving.

In the end, the treasure of life is missed by those who try to hold on to it, and it's gained by those who let it go.

Life is a series of natural and spontaneous changes. Don't resist them; that only leads to sorrow.

Let reality be reality.

Stop seeking and you will receive.

Rejoice in the way things are.

When you realize there is nothing lacking, the whole world belongs to you.

The person who stands on tiptoe doesn't stand firm.

The person who rushes ahead doesn't go far.

Just do your job, then let go.

#35

CHOOSE HAPPY

Joyfulness is a choice you make every day.

Happiness is a choice, not a result.
Nothing will make you happy until you choose to be happy.
No person will make you happy unless you decide to be happy.
Your happiness will not come to you.
It can only come from you.

—RALPH MARSTON

We can all live our Best Day Ever each day of our lives. It's not some happy slogan I chant just because I like the sound of it. Happiness is a choice—and we can choose to be happy every single day.

The way that happens is by making small deliberate choices. Did you choose to have that extra drink last night? Did you turn off the light and go to bed a half an hour earlier so you got seven hours of sleep instead of six-and-a-half hours of sleep? Did you hold your tongue when you wanted to snap at someone, so that you had a better, easier day? How did you choose to act when someone criticized you this morning? Did you take it personally or did you move on? Each and every day offers us a series of these small choices. We can't control all of life's circumstances—but how we respond to them is completely up to us. We can choose to grow instead of stagnate or turn back; we can choose to learn, so that we have more power and freedom; and we can use both discipline and creativity to purposefully build a life of happiness and success. For me, this means practicing the strategies I've described in this book—doing them consciously and deliberately until they've become my fallback habits.

There's scientific evidence that Best-Day living is possible. Research has found that we can actually change the physical structure of our brains by what we choose to focus our attention on—and these neural changes will make us happier and more positive about life in general. It's called "self-directed neuroplasticity."

Neuroplasticity refers to the malleable nature of the brain. Scientists used to believe that brain cells couldn't be changed once they were formed. Whatever brain cells we had was what we got for the rest of our lives. But more recent research has proven that brain cells are constantly changing. Self-directed neuroplasticity means making that ongoing process happen with deliberate skillfulness and intention.

The key to doing this, scientists say, is being intentional about how we use our attention. For example, if we rest our attention routinely on things that we resent or that frustrate us, then we build a neural network around those thoughts and feelings. That network makes it easier and easier to feel upset and angry—and more and more difficult to react positively. On the other hand, if we choose to focus our attention on the things for which we're grateful and all the other positive things in our lives, then we build very different neural networks. Those networks then make it easier and easier to feel positive about life in general. They make constructive responses come more easily.

There are also a couple of ways you can trick your body into feeling happy. Physical activity gets our endorphins going (the brain's natural feel-good chemicals), so there's an immediate happiness payoff. In fact, scientific studies have found that exercise can be as effective or even more effective than antidepressant medications for lifting our mood.

You can also paste a smile to your face, no matter how you're feeling inside. Buddhist teacher Thich Nhat Hanh writes, "Sometimes your joy is the source of your smile, but sometimes your smile can be the source of your joy"—and he's absolutely right. Simply shifting your facial muscles into a smile floods your body with all the good hormones, such as endorphins and serotonin, that will lift your spirits. What's more, research has found that smiles are literally, physically contagious (in the same way that yawns are). When you smile at someone, it creates a physiological response in that person. They literally have to make a conscious effort *not* to smile back.

Each time you smile at people, their brains not only tell them to return the favor, but their brains are also flooding *their* bodies with feel-good chemicals. The simple decision to smile can make you and everyone around you happier and healthier.

So smile. Make it a habit. Consciously make other new habits that lead to a Best-Day-Ever life as well.

So, do you want to be happy—or not? It's *your* choice!

BUSINESS APPLICATION

Companies such as Zappos, Southwest Airlines, and Moo.com have found a new business model. It's called happiness. By making happiness their first priority— their own, their employees', and their customers'— they've created incredibly strong businesses.

We spend most of our waking lives at work, so it's important that we're happy there. Otherwise, we'll burn out. The businesses we just mentioned have found that one of the first steps to a successful business is finding and following your passion, the thing that will give your work life meaning. But don't only ask yourself, "What do I enjoy?" Instead, ask, "What problems do I see that need addressing that get me excited?" (See Strategy #1.)

Happiness makes us more effective at work. It keeps us focused, engaged, creative, and productive. Stress, boredom, and discouragement, however, can distract us, make it harder for us to make smart decisions, and cause us to overact to setbacks. Our brains become more alert, more open to new ideas and innovation when we're happy, which means we can work to our full potential.

Happiness is also contagious. If you're happy, then your employees are more likely to be happy too— and multiple studies have proven that happy teams are more creative, productive, and effective. As Zappos, Southwest, and Moo have discovered, happy employees then make happy customers. And although this isn't the goal—instead, it's a happiness side effect—happy customers spend more money, are more loyal to a brand, and spread the word. This means that happiness isn't only a business model. It's also a marketing plan!

MAKE IT PERSONAL

- Look back at the strategies in this book. Which ones have you tried?

- How did practicing these strategies affect your life?

- Pick one more strategy to begin consciously practicing this week. Describe what you will commit to doing to make this your new habit.

- After a week, review how successful you've been with your new practice. Has it worked for you? If not, what could you do differently? What other changes might you need to make in your life?

INSPIRATION

Malala Yousafzai was born into a culture where women were expected to be obedient. Women lacked many freedoms, including the right to an education. And yet Malala has always chosen happiness. Her choice, however, didn't mean that she was content to let things continue to be as they were. Instead, her joyous spirit gave her the courage to speak up and take action—despite the danger.

When she was ten, the Taliban had turned her home in Pakistan into a war zone. They controlled all forms of media; they closed schools; they raided houses and kidnapped women; they shut down businesses; they threw books, CDs, televisions, and computers into bonfires; they publicly whipped and beat people they deemed to be disobedient; they blew up buildings, museums, and houses; and they murdered anyone who actively resisted.

Not a good environment for happiness! But both Malala and her father took joyful action. They stood up and spoke out against the Taliban's injustice. Her father had always been an advocate for education, and now he and his daughter became outspoken opponents of the Taliban's efforts to restrict education and stop girls from going to school. When Malala was just fourteen, she received Pakistan's National Youth Peace Prize and was nominated by Archbishop Desmond Tutu for the International Children's Peace Prize.

In response to her rising popularity and recognition, Taliban leaders voted to kill Malala. The following year, when she was fifteen, a Taliban gunman boarded her school bus, asked for her by name, and gunned her down. She was not expected to survive, but doctors in the UK performed brain surgery, attaching a metal plate to her skull and a cochlear implant to restore hearing to her left ear. Part of her face remains paralyzed.

Malala didn't let that stop her. She became a global advocate for the millions of girls being denied a formal education because of social, economic, legal, and political factors. She and her father cofounded the Malala Fund to empower girls. Then, when Malala was seventeen, she became the youngest person to be awarded the Nobel Peace Prize. She contributed her entire prize money of more than $500,000 to financing the creation of a secondary school for girls in Pakistan.

If you see Malala speak, you'll hear and see the joy that's like a flame inside her. Her father says that his daughter is "the spirit of happiness." And Malala's goal is to spread happiness to others. She says that her goal is "education for every boy and every girl in the world . . . . To see each and every human being with a smile of happiness is my wish."

If Malala can choose happiness, despite the horrifying challenges she's faced, so can we. We don't need to win the Nobel Peace Prize for our happiness to make a difference in the world.

FURTHER READING AND VIEWING LIST

STRATEGY #1

Keller, Helen. *The Story of My Life*. Mineola, NY: Dover Publications, 2012 (reprint).

Stone Zander, Rosamund, and Benjamin Zander. *The Art of Possibility: Transforming Professional and Personal Life*. New York: Penguin Books, 2002.

STRATEGY #2

Branson, Richard. n.d. "The Importance of Passion in Business." *Virgin.com*. www.virgin.com/entrepreneur/richard-branson-the-importance-of-passion-in-business.

Paquette, Jonah. *Real Happiness: Proven Paths for Contentment, Peace & Well-Being*. Eau Claire, WI: PESI Publishing, 2015.

STRATEGY #3

American Psychological Association. "What Americans Think of Willpower: A Survey of Perceptions of Willpower & Its Role in Achieving Lifestyle and Behavior-Change Goals." *American Psychological Association*. 2012. www.apa.org/helpcenter/stress-willpower.pdf.

American Psychological Association. n.d. "What You Need to Know about Willpower: The Psychological Science of Self-Control." *American Psychological Association*. www.apa.org/helpcenter/willpower.aspx.

Cooper, Belle Beth. "6 Scientifically Proven Ways to Boost Your Self-Control." *FastCompany.com*. 2014. www.fastcompany.com/3032513/work-smart/6-scientifically-proven-ways-to-boost-your-self-control.

Cummins, Dennis. "How to Boost Your Willpower." *Psychology Today*. 2013. www.psychologytoday.com/blog/good-thinking/201306/how-boost-your-willpower.

Evans, Lisa. "The Power of Mornings: Why Successful Entrepreneurs Get Up Early." *Entrepreneur*. 2013. www.entrepreneur.com/article/226910.

Friesa, Malte, Claude Messnerb, and Yves Schaffnera. "Mindfulness Meditation Counteracts Self-Control Depletion." *Science Direct.com*. 2012. www.sciencedirect.com/science/article/pii/S1053810012000104.

Macur, Juliet. "Once Told He'd Never Walk Again, Irish Gymnast Is Now Olympian." *New York Times,* July 26, 2012.

STRATEGY #4

Amabile, Teresa, and Steven J. Kramer. "The Power of Small Wins." *Harvard Business Review*, May 2011.

Duhigg, Charles. *The Power of Habit: Why We Do What We Do in Life and Business*. New York: Random House, 2012.

STRATEGY #5

Clear, James. "How to Stick with Good Habits Every Day by Using the 'Paper Clip Strategy.'" *James Clear*. 2015. http://jamesclear.com/paper-clips.

O'Mahony, John. "When Less Means More." *The Guardian*. 2001. www.theguardian.com/education/2001/nov/24/arts.highereducation1.

STRATEGY #7

Keenan, Jim. "The Proven Predictor of Sales Success Few Are Using." *Forbes*. 2015. www.forbes.com/sites/jimkeenan/2015/12/05/the-proven-predictor-of-sales-success-few-are-using/#5d1eb0fa5d60.

McGinnis, Alan Loy. *The Power of Optimism*. New York: HarperCollins, 1990.

Martin E. P. Seligman has written several excellent books on the power of optimism, including *Authentic Happiness: Using the New Positive Psychology to Realize Your Potential for Lasting Fulfillment* (Free Press, 2002), *Learned Optimism: How to Change Your Mind and Your Life* (Random House, 2011), and *Flourish: A Visionary New Understanding of Happiness and Well-being* (Simon & Schuster, 2011).

STRATEGY #8

Danner, John, and Mark Coopersmith. *The Other "F" Word: How Smart Leaders, Teams, and Entrepreneurs Put Failure to Work*. New York: Wiley, 2015.

Whitworth, William. "Kentucky Fried." *New Yorker Magazine*, February 14, 1970.

STRATEGY #9

Rao, Srikumar S. *Are You Ready to Succeed?: Unconventional Strategies to Achieving Personal Mastery in Business and Life*. New York: Hachette, 2006.

Roberts, Travis. "'Burn the Ships!'—A Leadership Lesson from Cortés." *travisroberts.com*. 2010. http://travisrobertson.com/leadership/burn-ships-succeed-die/.

STRATEGY #10

Dooley, Roger. "How Warren Buffett Avoids Getting Trapped by Confirmation Bias." *Forbes*. 2013. www.forbes.com/sites/rogerdooley/2013/05/07/buffett-confirmation-bias/#7546bca3a838.

Kaplan, Robert E., and Robert B. Kaiser. "Stop Overdoing Your Strengths." *Harvard Business Review*. 2009. https://hbr.org/2009/02/stop-overdoing-your-strengths.

Nickerson, Raymond S. "Confirmation Bias: A Ubiquitous Phenomenon in Many Guises." *Review of General Psychology*. 1998. http://psy2.ucsd.edu/~mckenzie/nickersonConfirmationBias.pdf.

Rockwell, Dan. n.d. *Leadership Freak*. https://leadershipfreak.wordpress.com/.

STRATEGY #11

Covey, Steven. *The 7 Habits of Highly Effective People: Powerful Lessons in Personal Change*. New York: Simon & Schuster, 2013 (reprint).

Sinek, Simon. *Start with Why: How Great Leaders Inspire Everyone to Take Action*. New York: Penguin, 2009.

Sinek, Simon. *Ted Talk*. 2013. www.youtube.com/watch?v=sioZd3AxmnE.

STRATEGY #12

Kinomura, Shigeo, Jonas Larsson, Balázs Gulyás, and Per E. Roland. "Activation by Attention of the Human Reticular Formation and Thalamic Intralaminar Nuclei." *Science*. 1996. http://science.sciencemag.org/content/271/5248/512.

Leaf, Caroline. *Switch On Your Brain: The Key to Peak Happiness, Thinking, and Health*. Ada Township, MI: Baker, 2013.

Mayberry, Matt. "The Extraordinary Power of Visualizing Success." *Entrepreneur*, January 30, 2015.

Niles, Frank. "How to Use Visualization to Achieve Your Goals." *Huffington Post*. 2011. www.huffingtonpost.com/frank-niles-phd/visualization-goals_b_878424.html.

Shallard, Peter. n.d. "Why Having a Mission Changes All the Rules." *Peter Shallard*. www.petershallard.com/procrastination-is-perfect-why-having-a-mission-changes-all-the-rules/.

Sheikh, Anees A. *Imagery in Sports and Physical Performance*. Amityville, NY: Baywood, 1994.

STRATEGY #13

Palmer, Parker. *Let Your Life Speak*. New York: Jossey-Bass, 2009.

Walker, TW. *Superhero Success*. London, UK: Breakthrough Media, 2012.

STRATEGY #14

Gollwitzer, Peter M. "Striving for Specific Identities: The Social Reality of Self-Symbolizing." 1986. *NYU Department of Psychology*. www.psych. nyu.edu/gollwitzer/86Goll_SpecificIdentities.pdf.

Gollwitzer, Peter M., Paschal Sheeran, Verena Michalski, and Andrea E. Seifert. "When Intentions Go Public: Does Social Reality Widen the Intention-Behavior Gap?" *Psychological Science*. 2009. www.psych. nyu.edu/gollwitzer/09_Gollwitzer_Sheeran_Seifert_Michalski_When_Intentions_.pdf.

Harnish, Verne. "Quarterly Themes—Driving Focus." *Growth Guy*. 2008. www.gazelles.com/columns/Quarterly%20Themes.pdf.

Renando, Chad. "A Way to Map a Path to Your Goals, Using Kurt Lewin's Field Theory." *Sideways Thoughts*. 2015. www.sidewaysthoughts. com/blog/2015/03/a-way-to-map-a-path-to-your-goals-using-kurt-lewins-field-theory/.

Sivers, Derek. "Keep Your Goals to Yourself." *Ted Talk*. 2010. www.ted. com/talks/derek_sivers_keep_your_goals_to_yourself.

STRATEGY #15

Galindo, Linda. *The 85% Solution: How Personal Accountability Guarantees Success*. New York: Jossey-Bass, 2009.

Stringer, Leigh. *The Healthy Workplace: How to Improve the Well-Being of Your Employees—And Boost Your Company's Bottom Line*. AMACON, 2016.

STRATEGY #16

Bateman, Thomas, and Bruce Berry. "Masters of the Long Haul." *Journal of Organizational Behavior* 33(7). 2012.

NASA. n.d. *New Horizons.* www.nasa.gov/mission_pages/newhorizons/main/index.html.

Williams, Jennifer. "Examples of Long- & Short-Term Goals for a Business." *Chron*, January 10, 2017.

STRATEGY #17

Covey, Steven. *The 7 Habits of Highly Effective People: Powerful Lessons in Personal Change.* New York: Simon & Schuster, 2013 (reprint).

Tracy, Brian. *Eat That Frog!: 21 Great Ways to Stop Procrastinating and Get More Done in Less Time.* Oakland, CA: Berrett-Koehler, 2007.

STRATEGY #18

Copeland, Michael V. "You Can't Improve What You Can't Measure." *Wired.* 2012. www.wired.com/2012/05/nike-olander/.

Hardy, Darren. *The Compound Effect.* New York: Vanguard, 2011.

STRATEGY #19

Borreli, Lizette. "Why Using Pen And Paper, Not Laptops, Boosts Memory: Writing Notes Helps Recall Concepts, Ability To Understand." *Medical Daily.* 2014. www.medicaldaily.com/why-using-pen-and-paper-not-laptops-boosts-memory-writing-notes-helps-recall-concepts-ability-268770.

Clear, James. n.d. "Achieve Your Goals: Research Reveals a Simple Trick That Doubles Your Chances for Success," *James Clear*. http://jamesclear.com/implementation-intentions.

May, Cindi. "A Learning Secret: Don't Take Notes with a Laptop." *Scientific American*. 2014. www.scientificamerican.com/article/a-learning-secret-don-t-take-notes-with-a-laptop/.

Milne, Sarah, Sheina Orbell, and Paschal Sheeran. "Combining Motivational and Volitional Interventions to Promote Exercise Participation: Protection Motivation Theory and Implementation Intentions." *British Journal of Health Psychology*. 2010. http://onlinelibrary.wiley.com/doi/10.1348/135910702169420/abstract.

Quittner, Jeremy. "Small-Business Owners Brace for Hurricane Isaac." *Inc*. 2012. www.inc.com/jeremy-quittner/small-business-disaster-preparedness-insurance-hurricane-isaac.html.

US Small Business Administration. n.d. *Disaster Planning*. www.sba.gov/managing-business/running-business/emergency-preparedness/disaster-planning.

Vanderkam, Laura. *What the Most Successful People Do Before Breakfast: And Two Other Short Guides to Achieving More at Work and at Home*. New York: Portfolio, 2013.

STRATEGY #20

Villano, Matt. "5 Tips for Maintaining Work-Life Balance, From People Who've Been There." *Entrepreneur*. 2016. www.entrepreneur.com/article/253635.

STRATEGY #21

Adams, Laura D. *Money Girl's Smart Moves to Deal with Your Debt (Quick & Dirty Tips)*. New York: St. Martin's Griffin, 2010.

Harnish, Verne. *Scaling Up: How a Few Companies Make It . . . and Why the Rest Don't (Mastering Rockefeller Habits 2.0)*. Gazelles Publishing, 2014.

STRATEGY #22

AAA Foundation for Traffic Safety. n.d. "Sleep Deprivation and Crash Risk." *AAA Foundation for Traffic Safety*. www.aaafoundation.org/acute-sleep-deprivation-and-crash-risk.

Beccutia, Guglielmo, and Silvana Pannaina. "Sleep and Obesity." *Current Opinion in Clinical Nutrition and Metabolic Care*. 2011. www.ncbi.nlm.nih.gov/pmc/articles/PMC3632337/.

Czeisler, Charles A., and Bronwyn Fryer. "Sleep Deficit: The Performance Killer, A Conversation with Harvard Medical School Professor Charles A. Czeisler." *Harvard Business Review*, October 1, 2006.

Harvard Medical School. "Blue Light Has a Dark Side." *Harvard Health Publications*. 2015. www.health.harvard.edu/staying-healthy/blue-light-has-a-dark-side.

Harvard Medical School. n.d. "Why Sleep Matters." *Healthy Sleep*. http://healthysleep.med.harvard.edu/video/sleep07_matters.

Heffron, Thomas M. "Sleep and Caffeine." *American Academy of Sleep Medicine*. 2013. www.sleepeducation.org/news/2013/08/01/sleep-and-caffeine.

National Sleep Foundation. n.d. "How Much Sleep Do We Really Need?" *National Sleep Foundation.* https://sleepfoundation.org/how-sleep-works/how-much-sleep-do-we-really-need.

Rosenthal, Joshua. *Integrative Nutrition: Feed Your Hunger for Health and Happiness (Third Edition).* New York: Integrative Nutrition, 2014.

US National Heart, Blood, and Lung Institute. "Why Is Sleep Important?" *US National Heart, Blood, and Lung Institute.* 2012. www.nhlbi.nih.gov/health/health-topics/topics/sdd/why.

van Dam, Nick, and Els van der Helm. "The Organizational Cost of Insufficient Sleep." *McKinsey Quarterly.* 2016. www.mckinsey.com/business-functions/organization/our-insights/the-organizational-cost-of-insufficient-sleep.

STRATEGY #23

Ahmed, S. H., K. Guillem, and Y. Vandaele. "Sugar Addiction: Pushing the Drug-Sugar Analogy to the Limit." *Current Opinion in Clinical Nutrition and Metabolism Care,* 2013, 16(4). doi: 10.1097/MCO.0b013e328361c8b8.

Health Enhancement Research Organization. "New Findings and Realistic Solutions to Employee Presenteeism." *Health Enhancement Research Organization (HERO).* 2014. http://hero-health.org/wp-content/uploads/2014/03/Presenteeism_white_paper.pdf.

International Labor Organization. "Decent Food at Work: Raising Workers' Productivity and Well-Being." *International Labour Organization.* 2008. www.ilo.org/global/about-the-ilo/newsroom/news/WCMS_075505/lang-en/index.htm.

Kaiser Permanente. "Keeping a Food Diary Doubles Diet Weight Loss, Study Suggests." *Science Daily.* 2008. www.sciencedaily.com/releases/2008/07/080708080738.htm.

Polan, Michael. *The Omnivore's Dilemma: A Natural History of Four Meals.* New York: Penguin, 2006.

Wolpert, Stuart. "Scientists Learn How What You Eat Affects Your Brain — And Those of Your Kids." *UCLA Newsroom.* 2008. http://newsroom.ucla.edu/releases/scientists-learn-how-food-affects-52668.

STRATEGY #24

Coulson, J. C., J. McKenna, and M. Field. "Exercising at Work and Self-Reported Work Performance." *International Journal of Workplace Health Management.* 2008, 1(3). http://dx.doi.org/10.1108/17538350810926534.

Duhigg, Charles. *The Power of Habit: Why We Do What We Do in Life and Business.* New York: Random House, 2012.

Harmon, Katherine. "Social Ties Boost Survival by 50 Percent." *Scientific American.* 2010. www.scientificamerican.com/article/relationships-boost-survival/.

Reynolds, Gretchen. "What's the Value of Exercise? $2,500." *New York Times.* 2016. www.nytimes.com/2016/09/07/well/move/whats-the-value-of-exercise-2500.html.

Umberson, Debra, and Jennifer Karas Montez. "Social Relationships and Health: A Flashpoint for Health Policy." *Journal of Health and Social Behavior.* 2010. www.ncbi.nlm.nih.gov/pmc/articles/PMC3150158/.

Weinberg, "Goal Setting in Sport and Exercise." *Revista de Psicologia del Deporte.* 2007. www.rpd-online.com/article/download/61/61.

Weir, Kirsten. "The Exercise Effect." *American Psychological Association Monitor.* 2011. www.apa.org/monitor/2011/12/exercise.aspx.

STRATEGY #25

Ahlin, E. M. *Youth Involvement in Crime: The Importance of Locus of Control and Collective Efficacy.* El Paso, TX: LFB Scholarly Publishing, 2013.

Ahlin, E. M. "Locus of Control Redux." *Journal of Interpersonal Violence.* 2014, 29(14).

April, K. A., B. Dharani, and K. Peters. "Impact of Locus of Control Expectancy on Level of Well-Being." *Review of European Studies.* 2012, 4(2).

Blanchard, Richard. "Be Responsible for Your Success with an Internal Locus of Control." *Corp!.* 2012. www.corpmagazine.com/executives-entrepreneurs/expert-advice/be-responsible-for-your-success-with-an-internal-locus-of-control/.

Neymotin, Florence, and Louis R. Nemzer. "Locus of Control and Obesity." *Frontiers in Endocrinology.* 2014. doi: 10.3389/fendo.2014.00159.

Tracy, Ben. "Refugee Swimmer Yusra Mardini Makes History in Olympic Pool." *CBS News.* 2016. www.cbsnews.com/news/refugee-swimmer-yusra-mardini-makes-history-in-rio-olympic-pool/.

STRATEGY #26

Margolis, Joshua D., and Paul Stoltz. "How to Bounce Back from Adversity." *Harvard Business Review.* 2010. https://hbr.org/2010/01/how-to-bounce-back-from-adversity.

STRATEGY #27

Fishman, Ted C. "Don't Underestimate the Power of Friendship." *USATODAY.* 2015. www.usatoday.com/story/opinion/2015/06/07/friendship-science-human-needs-column/26633027/.

O'Connor, Anahad. "The Secrets to a Happy Life, From a Harvard Study." *New York Times*, March 23, 2016.

Seppala, Emma, and Kim Cameron. "Proof That Positive Work Cultures Are More Productive." *Harvard Business Review.* 2015. https://hbr.org/2015/12/proof-that-positive-work-cultures-are-more-productive.

STRATEGY #28

Achor, Shawn, and Michelle Gielan. "Consuming Negative News Can Make You Less Effective at Work." *Harvard Business Review*, September 14, 2015.

Hutt, Rosamond. "9 Novels That Changed the World." *World Economic Forum.* 2016. www.weforum.org/agenda/2016/03/10-novels-that-changed-the-world/.

STRATEGY #29

Branson, Richard. "Change," *Virgin.com*. 2015. www.virgin.com/ richard-branson/my-top-10-quotes-on-change.

Isaac, Anna. "The 10 essential qualities of a modern marketer." *The Telegraph*. 2016. www.telegraph.co.uk/connect/media-and-technology/ ten-qualities-modern-marketers-must-have/.

Slingerland, Edward Gilman III. n.d. "Trying Not to Try." *TED Talk*. http://eslingerland.arts.ubc.ca/.

Twose, Helen. "Workers Need to Go with the Flow." *New Zealand Herald*. 2016. http://m.nzherald.co.nz/business/news/article. cfm?c_id=3&objectid=11704436.

Tierney, John. "A Meditation on the Art of Not Trying." *New York Times*, December 15, 2014, https://www.nytimes.com/2014/12/16/ science/a-meditation-on-the-art-of-not-trying.html.

STRATEGY #30

Algoe, Sara B., Shelly L. Gable, and Natalya C. Maisel. "It's the Little Things: Everyday Gratitude as a Booster Shot for Romantic Relationships." *Personal Relationships*. 2010. http://ggsc-web02.ist.berkeley.edu/ images/application_uploads/ Algoe-GratitudeAndRomance.pdf.

Dunn, Lauren. "Be Thankful: Science Says Gratitude Is Good for Your Health." *Today*. 2016. www.today.com/health/be-thankful-science-says-gratitude-good-your-health-t58256.

Gino, Francesca, and Adam Grant. "The Big Benefits of a Little Thanks." *Harvard Business Review*. 2013. https://hbr.org/2013/11/ the-big-benefits-of-a-little-thanks.

Kralik, John. *A Simple Act of Gratitude: How Learning to Say Thank You Changed My Life*. New York: Hachette, 2011.

Ruiz, Don Miguel. *The Four Agreements: A Practical Guide to Personal Freedom (A Toltec Wisdom Book)*. San Rafael, CA: Amber-Allen, 2011.

University of Berkeley. n.d. "Expanding the Science and Practice of Gratitude." *Greater Good Science Center*. http://greatergood.berkeley.edu/expandinggratitude.

Winfrey, Oprah. "Oprah Talks to Elie Wiesel." *O: The Oprah Magazine*. 2000. www.oprah.com/omagazine/Oprah-Interviews-Elie-Wiesel.

STRATEGY #31

Amen, Daniel G. *Change Your Brain, Change Your Life: The Breakthrough Program for Conquering Anxiety, Depression, Obsessiveness, Lack of Focus, Anger, and Memory Problems*. New York: Random House, 2015.

Evans, Lisa. "A Psychologist Shares One Surprising Way to Boost Your Confidence." *Business Insider*. 2015. www.businessinsider.com/psychologist-shares-surprising-way-to-boost-confidence-2015-11.

Sequin, Molly. "One Simple Habit Could Make You More Successful." *Business Insider*. 2016. www.businessinsider.com/talking-to-yourself-could-be-beneficial-to-your-s-2016-7.

STRATEGY #32

Carsrud, Alan L., and Malin Brännback. *Understanding the Entrepreneurial Mind: Opening the Black Box*. New York: Springer, 2019.

Porter, Eleanor H. *Pollyanna*. London, UK: Hesperus, 2014 (reprint).

STRATEGY #33

Benson, Etienne. "The Many Faces of Perfectionism." *Monitor on Psychology*, November 2003.

Hewitt, Paul L. *Perfectionism: A Relational Approach to Conceptualization, Assessment, and Treatment.* New York: Guilford, 2017.

Lombardo, Elizabeth. "How to Overcome Perfectionism to Succeed in Business." *Entrepreneur.* 2014. www.entrepreneur.com/article/238268.

Nightingale, Robert. "The 10,000 Hour Rule Is Wrong. How to Really Master a Skill." *MakeUseOf.* 2015. www.makeuseof.com/tag/10000-hour-rule-wrong-really-master-skill/.

Schawbel, Dan. "Brené Brown: How Vulnerability Can Make Our Lives Better." *Forbes.* 2013. www.forbes.com/sites/danschawbel/2013/04/21/brene-brown-how-vulnerability-can-make-our-lives-better/#1dcf6b5560ba.

STRATEGY #34

Business Insider. "14 Virgin Companies That Even Richard Branson Could Not Stop Going Bust," *Business Insider.* 2016. www.businessinsider.com/richard-branson-fails-virgin-companies-that-went-bust-2016-5/#student-magazine-branson-dropped-out-of-school-at-16-to-start-a-magazine-called-student-1.

Kayes, D. Christopher. *Destructive Goal Pursuit: The Mount Everest Disaster.* New York: Macmillan, 2006.

STRATEGY #35

Hanson, Rick. "How to Trick Your Brain for Happiness." *Greater Good: The Science of a Meaningful Life.* 2011. http://greatergood.berkeley.edu/article/item/how_to_trick_your_brain_for_happiness.

The Nobel Foundation. "Malala Yousafzai Biography." *Nobel Prize.* 2014. www.nobelprize.org/nobel_prizes/peace/laureates/2014/yousafzai-bio.html.

BRAMBLE BERRY HANDCRAFT PROVISIONS
has everything you need to get creative and make products that are both beautiful and functional. Whether you've been wanting to make soap from scratch or whip up a moisturizing body butter, we've got you covered. In addition to thoroughly-tested products and easy-to-follow recipes, we also offer help every step of the way. We'll be your partner on your creative journey.

The best handcraft provisions

BrambleBerry.com has the supplies you need to make handmade products from start to finish, including essential oils, natural colorants, exfoliants, bottles, decorative boxes and even printable labels. Each one has been thoroughly tested by expert crafters to ensure it works well for you. The website also has resources to help you get started, including a Fragrance Calculator and Lye Calculator. Head over to BrambleBerry.com to get started on your creative journey.

Top-notch customer service

Our friendly and knowledgeable customer service team is happy to answer any questions you have about products, orders, or making handmade goods from scratch. You can reach us at 877-627-7883 between 9 a.m. and 4 p.m. PST, email info@brambleberry.com or chat on BrambleBerry.com from 9:30 a.m. to 3:30 p.m.

Hundreds of free recipes

Visit SoapQueen.com and you'll find recipes for melt and pour soap, cold process soap, lotion, lip balm, bath bombs and more. The posts have easy-to-understand instructions and pictures so your recipes turn out great each time. Make sure to check out SoapQueen.tv as well, which has more fun recipes for you to try.

Savvy small business advice

We are passionate about small business. SoapQueen.com offers tips to new business owners like how to label your products, where to sell them and how to set up an Etsy shop. There is also advice for seasoned business owners, including marketing on social media and how to start wholesaling your products.

Help and support from the crafting community

There's nothing better than showing off a product you're proud of with fellow crafters! Share your lovely creations using #SoapShare and get inspiration at:

www.facebook.com/BrambleBerry
www.instagram.com/brambleberry
twitter.com/brambleberry
www.pinterest.com/brambleberry